The Book of

NO

365 Ways to Say It, Mean It, and Stop People-Pleasing Forever

SECOND EDITION

Susan Newman, PhD
with Cristina Schreil

Other Books by Susan Newman

Praise for the Book of NO

"A colossal, common, and vexing problem, which causes many other devilishly inescapable problems, is not saying 'no' before 'yes' leaps out of your mouth. In this priceless, practical, pithy volume, Dr. Susan Newman uses her wisdom, wiles, and wit to teach you—kind, nice, good, and giving person that you are—how to bow out gracefully, how to decline an offer without giving offense, and how to teach others to do the same thing. This book is a game-changer and a life saver!"

—Edward Hallowell, MD,
author of *Driven to Distraction* and other books

"If you want to be a good friend, team player, and nice person, but always seem to put yourself—and the things you want—last, *The Book of No* is for you. It helps break down the stigma and guilt associated with saying no, and provides hundreds of tips for exactly how to say it in specific circumstances and relationships. You'll learn the psychology behind why you get sucked into saying yes too often and what to do to stop."

—Alice Boyes, PhD,
author of *The Anxiety Toolkit: Strategies for Fine-Tuning Your Mind and Moving Past Your Stuck Points*

"*The Book of No* gives people the courage to stand up for themselves. Reading it is both helpful and a delight; you find yourself sighing with gratitude, feeling freer because you have the exact words to say 'no,' and thinking of who else in your life needs this book."

—Jody J. Foster, MD, MBA and Michelle T. Joy, MD,
coauthors of *The Schmuck in My Office: How to Deal Effectively with Difficult People at Work*

"Overwhelmed? Overextended? Stressed? *The Book of No* is a must-read for the pushover tendency in all of us who agree to most things asked of us. Leading relationship psychologist Susan Newman explains why you say yes too often and how to say no graciously without feeling guilty or offending. Think of it as your life preserver and go-to guide for navigating relationships with your friends, family, spouse, boss, coworkers, parents, kids…even strangers. You'll want to say yes to *The Book of No* and keep it close by."

—Michele Borba, EdD,
educational psychologist and author of *UnSelfie: Why Empathetic Kids Succeed in Our All-About-Me World*

"Does it have to be a fact of life that, as parents, it's next to impossible to say no to our children? Susan Newman guides parents out of their giving-in habit with toddlers, teens, even adult children with smart advice in situations you will recognize and relate to. If you're a 'yes' parent, you need *The Book of No* to help you stand firm through your parenting journey. It's healthy for you and your kids!"

—Amy McCready,
author of *The "Me, Me, Me" Epidemic: A Step-by-Step Guide to Raising Capable, Grateful Kids in an Over-Entitled World*

"In a world infected by instant gratification and murky boundaries, saying no—and sticking to it—is quickly becoming a lost art. The good news is that Susan Newman is here to help. Using detailed examples, humor, and actionable steps, Newman helps us explore our own obstacles to setting and maintaining healthy boundaries and empowers us to put an end to personal overload. In saying 'yes' to 'no,' we just might make a dent in putting an end to our current culture of busy."

—Katie Hurley, LCSW,
author of *No More Mean Girls* and *The Happy Kid Handbook*

"A wise and practical guide to living a life that fits your personal values, Susan Newman's newest book is a treasure trove of realistic scenarios and thoughtful responses to help you let go of commitments that leave you feeling resentful and depleted. Whether it's a whining child or a demanding acquaintance, a guilt-tripping relative or an unreasonable work colleague, *The Book of No* offers doable strategies for setting healthy boundaries so you can say 'Yes!' to the things that truly matter to you."

—Eileen Kennedy-Moore, PhD,
NJ psychologist, and coauthor of *Growing Friendships: A Kids' Guide to Making and Keeping Friends*

"For many of us, it's very difficult to say no. We're asked to take on extra assignments at work and help colleagues and clients with projects that might be outside our official job description. We're asked for favors by our friends, by our families, and sometimes even by our LinkedIn connections. And yes, it's nice to help, but we can end up overburdened. In *The Book of No*, Susan Newman offers great strategies and tips for learning to say no. This book is going to be my new go-to volume for putting a bit more 'no' in my life—and in the life of my clients, colleagues, and friends."

—Andy Molinsky, PhD, professor of Organizational Behavior and International Management, Brandeis University, and author of *Reach* and *Global Dexterity*

"All too often we find ourselves overworked and overstressed because we take on too much at work or at home. In short, we have trouble saying no! Dr. Susan Newman's book is an essential guide for those of us who are too agreeable, nice, or helpful, and really don't know how to set critical limits."

—Ronald E. Riggio, PhD, professor of Leadership and Organizational Psychology, Claremont McKenna College

For the millions of people who find themselves in millions of places doing millions of things they don't want to be doing—simply because they couldn't say no

Turner Publishing Company
Nashville, Tennessee
New York, New York
www.turnerpublishing.com

The Book of No: 365 Ways to Say It and Mean It—and Stop People-Pleasing Forever

Cover design: Maddie Cothren
Book design: Tim Holtz

Library of Congress Cataloging-in-Publication Data
Names: Newman, Susan, author. | Schreil, Cristina, author.
Title: The book of no : 365 ways to say it, mean it, and stop people-pleasing
  forever / Susan Newman, PhD with Cristina Schreil.
Description: Second Edition. | Nashville, Tennessee : Turner Publishing
  Company, [2017] | Revised edition of the author's The book of no : 250
  ways to say it-- and mean it-- and stop people-pleasing forever, c2006. |
  Includes bibliographical references and index.
Identifiers: LCCN 2017045582 (print) | LCCN 2017049660 (ebook) | ISBN
  9781683366928 (e-book) | ISBN 9781683366904 (pbk. : alk. paper)
Subjects: LCSH: Assertiveness (Psychology) | Social desirability.
Classification: LCC BF575.A85 (ebook) | LCC BF575.A85 N49 2017 (print) |
DDC
  158.2--dc23
LC record available at https://lccn.loc.gov/2017045582

Printed in the United States of America
17 18 19 20 10 9 8 7 6 5 4 3 2 1

Contents

Author's Note

Ten years after writing the first edition of *The Book of NO*, it still surprises me how good it feels to say no or its equivalent—"I'm on overload right now"; "That's not going to work for me"; I'm busy that day." More surprising is that saying no doesn't mean the end of the world. It won't cause my children to stop loving me, my friends to abandon me, or my colleagues to ignore me.

In the last decade or so, however, life has started to feel like a pressure cooker, with mounting requests and demands. Technology certainly ups the potential for conflicts—people expect immediate answers. For one reason or another, most of us are busier than ever.

One of the traps I realized is, like many people, I think I can do more than I can. Given an allotted number of hours to do everything, something's got to give. But what? I understood that I needed to change my thinking and do a better job of setting up and guarding my boundaries, because boundaries are key to not being an inveterate people-pleaser buried in an avalanche of to-dos.

Obviously, there will be instances when you have to or want to help out. *The Book of NO* was not created to justify the egomaniac who wants everything his or her way. Rather, it's for those of us—me included—who say yes too often. It's for people who kick themselves after agreeing to do something that, it turns out, didn't really require their compliance.

This edition is chock-full of new situations and research that explain why a *no* may be the best answer and offers more ways to say it without feeling guilty or damaging a relationship.

You'll start paying more attention to what is asked, how and when it is asked, and how quickly you respond—usually too fast in an effort to please, placate, or avoid hurting someone's feelings. I have every hope that in short order you can adapt to living happily ever after with *no* as a staple in your vocabulary.

The goal is to gain better command of the word *no* in handling requests for your time, talent, muscle, money, know-how, or presence that pull you in too many directions, add to your stress and eat up precious time. The insights and examples that follow will strengthen your resolve so you have time to do more for the people and things most important to you. And that means for *yourself* as well.

Introduction

We live in a world that currently lauds the power of *yes*. It's a trend: numerous blogs, self-help books, and even plots of novels and movies suggest that saying yes unlocks more from life. This thinking instructs particularly timid people looking for adventure or change to say yes over playing it safe. In that way, *yes* is often a good thing. There's nothing wrong with a *yes* when it moves you closer to your goals: finally taking that boxing class you've always wanted to but were too wary to sign up for, keeping peace in the family, or strategically shoring up your position in the workplace. At work, saying yes purportedly sends the message that you are a team player, supporting your group and increasing your value to the company. A *yes* is perfectly fine if it moves you forward in some way or makes you feel good.

But here's the issue: "Yes." "Sure." "No problem." The words are out of your mouth before the reality or the enormity of the commitment registers. You realize too late that you don't want or don't have the time to do what you've taken on. You neither wish to babysit for a friend's or sibling's children, nor do you have time to walk a neighbor's pesky dog every time she asks. You wonder how you got roped into an extra office assignment or making arrangements for a coworker's farewell party. "How does this happen to me so often?" you ask. If you're not wondering, maybe you should.

No, the word you repeated without the slightest hesitation at age two, seems problematical, if not impossible, in many of your interactions today. Time to reorient yourself to the word *no*. It has the power to bring equilibrium to your life and better manage your interactions. By keeping *no* at the front of your mind, you have both a plan and the ability to meet it. With *no, your* well-being becomes a priority.

Quiz: How Much of a People-Pleaser Are You?

Often, people who regularly respond to requests with a *yes* rather than a *no* don't recognize their willingness or selflessness as a hindrance to their own progress and happiness. This quiz assists you in seeing your personal yes-no predicament more clearly. Note what you respond to with a *yes* or "Oh, that's me!"

1. Do you find you don't have enough time to exercise, relax, get enough sleep, or accomplish what you set out to do?
2. Are you often unable to express yourself or ask for what you want?
3. Do you say yes and then regret committing to what was asked of you?
4. Do you feel guilty when you turn someone down?
5. Do you resent the person who asked?
6. Do you have a need to be loved or liked?
7. Do you feel duped or manipulated once you've agreed to help out?
8. Do some of your relationships feel one-sided? Do you find yourself asking, "What does this person do for *me*, if anything?"
9. Do people see you as someone who is always available?
10. Does your fear of missing a fun event or fear of being left out influence how you respond to invitations or plans to get together?
11. Do you seem to be the person called on to make personal sacrifices whenever there is a problem?
12. Do you wish to be seen as the responsible, reliable person?

13. Do you sometimes think, "I am not having fun anymore"?
14. Do you sometimes feel that you do too much for others and not enough for yourself?
15. Do you allow the opinions of others to determine your self-worth?

If you had more yeses than nos, you probably say yes too often—you have the "disease" to please.

The Disease to Please: Why You Say Yes

If you are someone who does things for others, leaving little to no time for yourself, and often feel at your wit's end, put yourself in the "people-pleaser" category. It could be that you've been people-pleasing all your adult life, aiding others who thrive being on the receiving end. Being cared for is what the takers in your life have come to expect. That alone places you high on the people-pleasing scale.

Or you may be reluctant to state your needs, and by not stating your needs, you're leaving the door open to saying yes. It could be you are a busy junkie: the more you can cram into a day, the happier you are, and the happier you are, the more likely you are to say yes. *Yes* is the default position for many overcommitted people. After all, busy people get things done, and the people in your life know it. Many busy people have a ton on their plates already and tend to rationalize, "What's one more task?"

Or you may be someone who avoids confrontation or unpleasantness. For you, *yes* is the path of least resistance and the way to avoid damaging your relationship with the asker.

Incessant yeses often stem from the inability to think clearly about what is being asked. Many label the millisecond it takes to agree as a weak moment: "I was having a bad day"; "I was in a bad mood"; "I didn't feel well; my guard wasn't up"; and a long list of other excuses. What keeps you from saying no is usually right below the surface of the question: an implied judgment, an unspoken, guilt-producing *should*, your own hesitation to offend or disappoint, or your fear of the asker's power or perceived "hold" on you.

Then there's the dangerous gray zone, filled with those things you have no strong feelings or opinion about. When in the gray zone, you're wishy-washy and undecided. Requests out of the blue can leave you floundering in murky waters. Until you pause long enough to analyze a situation, you will continue to be a yes-person.

Or you may say yes because you like being needed and have gotten into the habit of being amenable. You enjoy the feelings of being liked or loved that emanate from cooperating. Similarly, you may crave the approval that validates you and gives your self-esteem a boost. You thrive on appreciation when people say, "Thank you." In the extreme, saying yes becomes an addiction.

Perhaps you are driven to say yes too much because you fear you will miss something fun or important. Maybe you worry about being left out or abandoned. Your concern may be that people will judge you negatively if you refuse or don't show up.

In moderation, being available is a good thing. Self-sacrificing, on the other hand, is not. Yes-people become weighed down, feel torn, trapped, or taken advantage of, and are often annoyed with themselves for being easy marks. The damage of saying yes indiscriminately affects you much more than your refusals affect the people you turn down.

Male or female, you may be a people-pleaser simply because, while growing up, you were taught to be nurturing and caring. Saying yes is how you have been functioning for what seems like forever. You can change that.

No: A Learned Skill

Saying no may be completely uncharted territory—when you're a master of *yes*, you're a novice of *no*. For you, saying no means trying something entirely foreign. Think of the process as an adventure into the unknown, with delicious bounty at the end of the journey: a calmer, happier life, with you supervising it.

To master saying no, you may have to move out of your comfort zone. While saying no won't change your personality, it will help you assert yourself and put an end to that empty feeling in the pit of your stomach when you commit beyond your stamina or to the point of draining your emotional reserves. Over time and with practice, *no* will become your first option instead of a current, deeply ingrained propensity to say yes.

No is a word steeped in negativity, a perception ingrained from childhood. When you were a child, you had little difficulty shouting, "No!" but slowly the word *no* was drilled out of you. If you said no to sharing your toys as a toddler, you were sent to your room or a toy was taken away; as you got older and refused a parental rule or direction, you lost privileges. These early experiences translated into concrete fears about using the word *no*.

No doubt some of that apprehension carried over into your adult life. It takes time to start seeing the true power of *no*—to protect your time, balance your relationships, safeguard your health, and create *positive* change. Before you can fully embrace *no*, you have to understand why *no* is important.

You may be a person who has to be pushed and prodded, have your back against the wall, or be on serious overload before the thought of saying no enters your mind. Being on a yes-treadmill is an unhealthy place to be. A perpetual diet of yeses is depleting and not good for the mind or the body. Stress and frustration build; added stress can affect your sleep and temperament and lead to depression. Feeling "under the gun" too often can also cause stomachaches or headaches and contribute to habits, such as overeating or smoking, that some use to cope with stress. In short, by saying no more often, you keep your stress level in check, avoiding possible health complications.

Transforming how you think about yourself and your life, even your dreams, will change how you respond to requests. Take some time to consider what you want and how all you do for others is probably holding you back or, at the least, slowing you down. With defined goals, you will be better able to avoid unwanted interruptions that interfere or put barricades in your path. You will be less likely to go with the will of others, to be generous and supportive every time you are called upon.

Think of *no* as your assistant, your cheerleader, the vehicle to become your best self. Saying no improves your state of mind and frees you to stay on course—your course—and feel more purposeful.

Changing Your Thinking

Take a moment to consider the people in your life who rarely hesitate to say no when asked to do something. Note how they guard their time and have boundaries in place that they hardly ever alter. Make one of them your role model.

Saying yes doesn't make you a better person, nor does saying no mean you are a less caring individual. You can still be kind and empathic without agreeing to all that is asked of you. Forget about the "shoulds" that nag at your conscience, sap your energy, and swallow significant chunks of your day.

It's frustrating when you can't get to what you want on a given day or accomplish goals you had percolating for months, possibly years. Hours and days vanish in a flash of getting sidetracked. Understanding your own needs and moving them to the forefront stops you from agreeing to do things you find distressing or self-defeating.

You can't assert yourself or indicate your preferences until you know what they are. Figuring out these personal or work-related objectives is fundamental to reaching your goals. Maybe you want to learn or perfect your skills on a musical instrument or speaking a foreign language. Your aim may be as simple as getting more sleep or devoting less time to running errands for your mother-in-law, who might be perfectly capable of doing them herself. Maybe you enjoy gardening or sewing or want to join a book club or see more movies, but you never seem to get around to it.

Stop overcommitting. Give yourself permission to take time for yourself and eliminate the drudgery of having jam-packed days and nights. It's perfectly okay to say "me first." With changed thinking and goal-oriented direction, you'll be better able to stick to your agenda, and life will begin to feel more satisfying and rewarding. Spelling out what you hope to achieve automatically shores up boundaries and keeps your priorities straight.

Setting Boundaries

To stop people from overstepping your boundaries, plan for what you want and reserve steadfast time slots—your child's naptime, for example, or an hour when you get home from work, or after dinner. When someone makes a request, you will know you don't want to give up the time you've saved. It doesn't mean that you won't ever give up reserved time.

Make lists (daily, weekly, monthly, or long term) and make it a practice to check them before you agree to anything. Post your list where you can see it as a reminder: tape it on your desk or put it in your wallet—somewhere it's readily accessible to act as a sort of conscience. Better yet, memorize it so you will be more inclined to refuse requests that prevent you from removing items from the list.

Equally effective: think about the things you want to stop doing. Jot them down to remind yourself.

Need more reinforcement? Post a "NO" sign on your computer or desk, near the phone you use regularly, in your kitchen—wherever you are most often and are most apt to be asked to do something.

Consider that each request may obliterate plans you've made. Answering these questions before you respond will reinforce your new attitude and better mark your boundaries:

- Do I have the time?
- What do I have to give up to do this?
- Will I feel pressured to get it done?
- Will I be upset with myself after saying yes?
- Will I resent the person asking?
- Will I feel duped, had, or coerced?
- Why am I agreeing? What's the gain?

Putting *No* to Work for You

The more comfortable you become saying no, the more opportunities you create to achieve the less chaotic, more fulfilling life that always seems just out of reach.

At times, maximizing the power of *no* requires understanding when to say yes, when to stand firm, or when it is wise to negotiate. You will learn how to make the best of a *no* answer—that is, refuse a request yet create the least amount of pushback when you do. You will be able to say no and still remain in the good graces of friends, family, work colleagues, and bosses. You will also have skills and planned responses to deal with extraneous harassing or especially persistent people.

Even after you make a commitment to yourself, you may need stronger boundaries in some areas more than others. Perhaps you have no difficulty refusing your partner, but saying no to your children is a whole other story. Decide where your boundaries are strong and where they need work.

You might choose to build your no-power with friends, and after reading chapter 2, "With Friends," you'll be able to meet them head-on. If your family pulls you into all things unimaginable, you'll want to focus on chapter 3, "All in the Family." If encounters and conflicts with your children call for refusals, you'll discover ways to navigate *no* as a parent in chapter 4, "With Children—Park Your Guilt." If your hesitancy to say no is most prevalent on the job, then survey chapter 5, "At Work," to learn scripts to use with your boss, coworkers, or clients. Delve into chapter 6, "Really Difficult People," to master *no* with an array of busybodies, salespeople, and scammers who hope that you will say yes or get sucked into their swindle.

Each chapter is filled with situations, questions, and demands that snag people every day. While a request may not be one precisely asked of you, you will recognize the predicament and start to think ahead to similar situations in which you might be caught off guard.

Scenarios include questions, requests, and demands. Each scenario is dissected into three parts: "What's Going on Here," "Response," and "Alert."

- **What's Going on Here:** This section warns of the possible motives behind the "ask," offering details of the circumstances that could influence how you respond. "What's Going on Here" analyzes what's asked and why you may have a hard time saying no. This knowledge builds resistance and helps assemble a strong base from which to begin your turnaround.

- **Response:** Responses help extricate you and, in most instances, suggest language to disengage you from the commitment without your seeming uninterested or impolite. When you aren't confident that you can find the words on your own, the scripts give you the words to say no. This also helps you assess the situation and answer less impulsively.

- **Alert:** The "Alert" provides rationale and words of caution so the next time you're in a similar bind you'll hesitate before locking yourself in. The "Alert" also reveals what people who ask favors think, why they behave the way they do to get you to do something for them, and in certain cases why you react as you do. This knowledge gives you the courage to say no without obsessing over the decision.

Some approaches to *no* may seem hard-edged, but they are realities of life. They are truths about others and ourselves that we don't want to accept and facts about human nature that are sometimes difficult to acknowledge. An important lesson to learn from the start is: *People don't think about you as much as you worry about what they think. As soon as you say no, they move on to find someone to do what they are asking.*

By saying no, you state your opinion, stand up for yourself, and become sole proprietor of your life. Begin by using a few refusals here and there as a testing ground. The first *no* to a person makes subsequent refusals easier. A short statement to express your denial is sufficient. Lengthy explanations leave wiggle room for debate or misinterpretation or can tacitly grant permission to ask again.

··· 1 ···

Stepping into *No*

The Basics

Saying no emphatically doesn't mean you are aggressive, obnoxious, selfish, or controlling. It means you know how to protect yourself. The alternative—when you can't help but say yes—often leaves you feeling deceived, frustrated, giving your all and not getting much in return, or being smothered, perpetually overworked, overextended, or tired.

Although it's easy to accuse others of asking too much, you could be at fault for expecting too much of yourself. Exercise your option to choose. In the world of *no*, reducing demands prevents you from choking on self-inflicted overload. Saying no is practicing self-defense, and self-defense is not selfish.

You won't be able to say no to everything asked of you, nor will you want to, but you can find a middle ground. You don't have to be an ever-accommodating yes-person to be loved, respected, and admired. Saying no is not only liberating—it is your right.

These six basic steps will hone your ability to turn people down. As soon as you begin to apply them, you will begin to feel justified saying no.

1. **Get your priorities straight.** Who has first crack at you without your feeling burdened or anxious? A child? A friend? A parent? A partner? A boss?

1

2. **Pay attention to how you parcel out your time.** If most of your time is monopolized assisting one friend, for example, when will you see other friends? If family or job demands are high, what's left over for your own enjoyment? When your time is well-managed, you keep some in reserve for what's important to you.

3. **Recognize when and how often you say yes.** Jot down your yeses over the period of a week. If you have yes-person tendencies, the number may shock you. The acceptable number is different for everyone. One request could send you into a tailspin, while it might take four or more to unhinge someone else. The real gauge is how pressured, tight for time, or upset you feel. Any negative reaction— "Why did I agree?" "What was I thinking!" "What am I doing?" "I would rather be elsewhere"—is the true measure.

4. **Stop trying to do it all.** The juggling act of being a loving partner, super-parent, or successful businessperson can be a lot for one person to manage. You may feel guilty when you can't be all things to all people and are compensating by being overly responsible and conscientious.

5. **Accept your limits.** Everyone has a set amount of physical and emotional energy. How much of other people's problems can you tolerate without feeling drained? How long are you willing to put up with lopsided relationships, with you always on the giving end? Decide how close you're willing to be and which kinds of requests make you uncomfortable or nervous. When does your physical stamina give out? What requests are too taxing or beyond your ability altogether? In order to stay healthy, the body and mind require rest to rejuvenate, and if you don't acknowledge your limits, you won't get it.

6. **Give control to others to minimize your responsibilities.** Discarding your need to "run the show," to be sure

everything turns out the way you like it, relieves much of the pressure you put on yourself and eliminates unnecessary yeses. If you are a perfectionist, when you don't trust others to be in charge or to get things accomplished, you wind up agreeing to and doing far more than your share.

Your Go-To *No* Responses

Harnessing the word *no* empowers you. When dodging requests, do not gild your *no* with a lie or pad it with lame excuses. Lies and excuses are counterproductive because in all likelihood you will feel guilty about your fabrications, and guilt is precisely what you are trying to avoid. Consider the list below your go-to response arsenal:

- I prefer not to . . .
- I'm uncomfortable . . .
- I'm not the right person . . .
- Regrettably, sadly, or unhappily, I can't . . .
- Wish I could, but . . .
- As much as I would like to help . . . Try me again another time.
- Maybe next time.
- Thank you for asking. I'm on overload.
- I have to think about that.

As you build your no-muscle, "Buying Time" and "When *No* Is Crystal Clear" are primer approaches you will want to remember. They will ease you into refusing the specific people examined in depth in later chapters.

Buying Time

Some things people ask of you require contemplation before giving a resounding *yes* or blatant *no*. This is that gray zone, so stay on your toes. The questions require you to be indirect or noncommittal initially. You'll want to digest what is being asked and to think about the outcome of your decision. Stalling tactics work to get you off the hook until you can be certain.

When you hedge a *no*, you buy extra time that makes your *no* more palatable and allows you to feel vindicated about not providing what the person wants. Given time, you might realize you don't want to be involved, you have no business giving an opinion, or these are people you don't want to help or respond to in any way—realizations that may not pop into your head when first approached. If nothing else, taking time to think things over makes the other person aware that you have reservations, and that alone may ward off future infringements. Being noncommittal or indirect puts an asker on notice.

··· SCENARIO ···

"Hey, can you help me with this?
It's driving me nuts."

What's Going on Here: You are off the clock, but your stressed-out coworker needs help with a task. You want to be a good sport but don't want to work during your break.

Response: "I need to do a few things before my break ends. Give me at least a half an hour."

Alert: Buying time works well in situations calling for your immediate aid. You're not bowing to someone else's timeline.

··· SCENARIO ···

*"Let's get a date on the calendar for
lunch or dinner, you name it."*

What's Going on Here: A casual acquaintance has been trying to lock you into a meal for a while. You are not as interested as he is. He's persistent and he gives you the entire calendar year from which to choose. If you make a date unwillingly, you'll spend a lot of time devising a way to break it.

Response: "I'm really busy and not sure what's coming up in the next month or two. I'll get back to you soon."

Alert: How you define the relationship is the determining factor. When it's someone you're lukewarm about, remind yourself that your life is rich with good friends you don't have time to see. If you stall someone over and over, at some point he will realize he's not on your radar screen.

··· SCENARIO ···

*"Kathryn and Bart are getting married.
Let's give them an engagement party at your
house, since it's bigger than ours."*

What's Going on Here: In the excitement, you're inclined to agree. It's wonderful that your good friends are finally tying the knot, and they should have a party. On happy occasions such as this, throwing a celebration shindig seems like a great idea—initially.

Response: "Let's talk about it."

Alert: In the heat of the moment, you may like the idea of being the person handling all the details. You may well end up throwing the party, but if you take time to think it through, you're less likely to take on more than you want to do.

··· SCENARIO ···

"Can I take violin lessons?"

What's Going on Here: In today's society, like adults, children are overscheduled. Musical instrument lessons on top of swimming and choir commitments are probably too much for your offspring. Two extracurricular activities per child per season are plenty.

Response: "We'll talk about it after swim season."

Alert: Parents need to buck the trend of organized activities to protect their children from overload and give them free time to play and explore—that's how children learn best.

··· SCENARIO ···

"Can I be your fourth for the front nine holes?"

What's Going on Here: This asker is a nice-enough guy off the golf course, but on it, he's a known cheat. Golfers who shave a stroke here and there make your blood boil. Isn't golf supposed to be relaxing, a game to enjoy with friends? Keep that in mind when you tell the cheat that he's not really welcome to play with your group.

Response: "I think Ted is our fourth; we usually play together." Or, "We're waiting for Ted" (if you are).

Alert: Including a cheat in a moment of weakness or guilt can ruin everyone's fun. Buying time is handy here—while you "wait for Ted," the annoying player will go in search of another group. If you foresee this happening again, arrange games in advance.

··· **SCENARIO** ···

"I've been so lonely since your dad died," your mom says. "Can I come stay with you for a while?"

What's Going on Here: You and your spouse have been speaking about how to navigate the best living situation for your mother, but her request catches you by surprise. While you and she have always clashed, you feel responsible for her. You worry how you'll be able to help your mother as she ages, especially if you live under one roof. Is "a while" even possible given your history?

Response: "Let's talk about options and make sure it's the best solution for everyone."

Alert: Caregiver burnout, a state of physical, mental, and emotional exhaustion, is a real issue. How dramatically will your family life change if a parent moves in? Will you be able to ensure you have alone time? Saying yes out of guilt or fear might lead to considerable stress and friction later on.

··· SCENARIO ···

*Your friend adds you to a text message thread
proposing a "HALLOWEEN BAR CRAWL!"
He adds, "If all five of us pitch in $30 up front,
we can get a special group rate on beer."*

What's Going on Here: Your buddy mentioned the idea a while back, but you weren't expecting something so involved. Frankly, it's a bit costly for you, considering you don't drink beer. He's counting on you for the discount, and you see that as the thread starts populating with the others agreeing.

Response: "I don't know if I'm in. I'll think about it."

Alert: The often fast-paced chatter of group texting can pressure you to act on the spot. Give it time and perhaps they will invite someone else to take your place. Then, if you end up going anyway, you can drink what you like.

··· SCENARIO ···

"Sam stormed out. I need you this minute."

What's Going on Here: Your friend sees you as the voice of reason, the person who can make sense of the breakup and make her feel better. She doesn't hear you tell her you're in the middle of cooking the first dinner for your in-laws or that the doctor told you to stop driving because you're nine months pregnant and can hardly get out of a chair. Your company may soothe her for the moment, but the real pain will return the minute you leave. Stopping what you are doing and rushing over immediately will not ease her distress, as you know from her many previous breakups.

Response: "I can't come over right now, but I'll call later to see how you're doing." Be sympathetic.

Alert: No one, certainly not a friend, can erase the pain of someone else's dissolving relationship. She'll sort it out in time. With persistent or manipulative people, you will simply have to repeat your *no* until they hear it.

··· SCENARIO ···

"Mom, I joined the ski team. We have to buy me new skis before Friday. The coach is giving us racing helmets."

What's Going on Here: Your child has perfectly fine skis and boots. He claims his skis are too short and not what he needs for racing. The cash register in your brain is on fast-forward as the requests mount. This child has a history of being enthusiastic only to have that passion wane fairly quickly.

Response: "Start with the equipment you have (or we'll rent what you need), and then we'll see about buying anything new."

Alert: Before you invest heavily in a child's new sport or hobby, make sure he's going to stick with it. Set up a trial period of several months, and when you're positive of his commitment, go on that shopping trip.

··· SCENARIO ···

"We're sailing the last weekend of next month. We need you to crew."

What's Going on Here: You love to sail and enjoy your sailing buddies, but the invitation puts you in conflict, as you have plans in the works for that same weekend. You don't want to be left out, but you also want to see your original plans through. If you say no immediately, they'll fill your slot with one phone call.

Response: "I have tentative plans. I'll let you know in a few days."

Alert: Try to keep options open so you don't wind up out on the water when you want to be elsewhere.

··· SCENARIO ···

You receive an online invitation for a charity ball. It reads in part: "Anyone who cares about the fight against breast cancer should attend."

What's Going on Here: You believe it's a great cause, but you don't have the money right now for such a grand event. You see many of your friends fill the "Attending" list and start to think you should do the same.

Response: Check the "Maybe" box. Write a message that underscores your support.

Alert: E-invites make it too easy to simply click and respond yes before you realize what you've signed up for. Remember, you can always donate money at a later date.

··· SCENARIO ···

*"I have to have it," your ten-year-old announces.
"You could buy it for my birthday."*

What's Going on Here: The latest game, tech gadget, or fashion "must" is undoubtedly the same one all his friends have or want.

Response: "Probably not, but I will think about it."

Alert: If you give your child every single gizmo he requests, what will he have to look forward to, and how will he learn to contribute, to work for what he wants? An unnecessary or expensive "want" that is the current craze—likely to be replaced by something else shortly—is a good place to draw the line.

··· SCENARIO ···

"Will you be in our wedding?"

What's Going on Here: In the midst of feeling flattered by the request, bridesmaids and groomsmen tend to accept on the spot without ruminating on some serious considerations: How close are you to the bride or groom? Can you afford to be in another wedding?

Response: "I'm honored you asked, but I have to see if I can swing it." This leaves you open to respond about work commitments or money problems or to decide being in the wedding party is too stressful.

Alert: Refusing doesn't mean the end of the friendship, but rather it means this isn't a good time for you. It would be far more damaging if you pulled out after plans were set. If you take your time before you commit, you are more likely to judge the situation accurately and be able to offer an unqualified *no*.

• • • • • • • • • • • •

When *No* Is Crystal Clear

You now have pointers for effective stalling, but in many instances a clear *no* is the strongest, most foolproof response. If you have been the most likely to help rectify situations in the past, it's logical you'd be approached again. An unmistakable *no* safeguards your energy and time while fostering a more even give-and-take.

At times you may feel boxed in, as if you have no choice, but remember: *you always have a choice.* What many people don't realize is that when you say no, the friend or neighbor, aunt, parent, or salesperson shifts gears; he or she wants her own needs satisfied and cares little for who comes to the rescue.

The encounters and dilemmas that follow help discriminate between what is a real need and what is only presented as such. You will learn how you can be useful without being overly involved. To combat any awkwardness that comes from a sudden swing from "Yes, of course" to a sure "No," reassure the person asking that you love or are fond of her or, if it applies, that you treasure or value the relationship.

··· SCENARIO ···

"Can I borrow your car for the weekend?
You said you had no plans."

What's Going on Here: Your friend may be in desperate need of a car, but how much will his or her borrowing it inconvenience you? Lending your means of transportation is asking a lot. What will you do if after your friend's use it needs to be repaired? Can you get by without your car? If this is a recurring request, consider the following before consenting: Is the car always returned with a full tank of gas? Is it as clean as it was when it left you? Is the borrower appropriately appreciative?

Response: "No, my policy is never to lend my car." Or, "I don't give up my car; I'm too dependent on it."

Alert: "Neither a borrower nor a lender be, / For loan oft loses both itself and friend" (William Shakespeare).

··· SCENARIO ···

You're at a restaurant (or anywhere), waiting for
one more person—the one who's always late. You
get a text: "Sorry I'm running late. Order for me?"

What's Going on Here: This person thinks his rudeness isn't a big deal. On top of everything, he expects you to act as his meal planner.

Response: "Nope. You can do that once you get here. We're starting without you."

Alert: Consistent tardiness is ill-mannered behavior that will only continue if left unchallenged. A clear *no* tells him that he's acting inappropriately and has to start respecting other people's time.

··· SCENARIO ···

Your parents exclaim, "You're not moving into that apartment, are you? We won't let you."

What's Going on Here: Many parents have a difficult time letting go of their independent, self-supporting adult children. They will look for, and find, flaws galore with any choice you make: the neighborhood is too dangerous, the space is too small, not enough closets, too noisy, too isolated, too far from us.

Response: "No, I have made up my mind. I love it."

Alert: Parents who harp can make you wonder if you are making the right choice. Don't allow parents' comments to undermine your confidence. When you know what you want to do, make the decision and tell them after the fact.

··· SCENARIO ···

"Will your wedding have hashtags on Instagram and Snapchat filters?" a friend asks.

What's Going on Here: You didn't go to the trouble of choosing a pricey wedding photographer to have your friends and family document your wedding via silly filters and blurry smartphone cameras. You want to ban phones altogether at your wedding to foster a sense of privacy, but you fear you'll come off like Bridezilla if you say something.

Response: "No, we really prefer a phone-free wedding to keep things intimate. There will be a place online to see the professional photographer's work after the wedding."

Alert: It's your wedding and while it's not realistic for you to be the phone police on the day of, letting guests know your wishes is your right.

··· SCENARIO ···

"Thanks for making dinner. I need to check my e-mail for one minute."

What's Going on Here: You've said that phones at the dinner table—especially for keeping an eye on work—irk you. You want to underscore that message but don't want a fight at the end of a long day.

Response: "You can put it away for at least twenty minutes while we eat. I deserve that."

Alert: Unless being in communication is a life-or-death matter for your partner, it's more crucial to respect each other's time and efforts.

··· SCENARIO ···

Your coworker asks, "Will you help me put together a speech for my meeting? It won't take long."

What's Going on Here: You know better. Before you can begin to be of any help, you will need to understand the background of the business, charity, or event, the focus of the speech, and information about the audience. That takes time.

Response: "No, I don't know anything about your project and don't have the time to learn it now."

Alert: Don't agree to do things for which the learning curve is too steep or too time-consuming, unless you see a strong and beneficial reason to do so.

••• SCENARIO •••

*"Will you write another letter to my
landlord? I don't know what to say, and
I've been trying to write it for days."*

What's Going on Here: Careful. The helpless approach can trip you up every time. Your first thought is, "How can I let this person down?" But, perhaps you've already written several letters for her. She's playing to your intellectual abilities, and you're buying.

Response: "No, but here's what you want to say . . ." Verbally give a few essential points to include in her next letter.

Alert: When left to their own devices, those who portray incompetence usually figure out what to do.

••• SCENARIO •••

*"We can clean and organize this dump in no time
if we each take a room. You start in the kitchen."*

What's Going on Here: You and a few friends or another couple signed a lease on a new apartment or summer rental. It needs elbow grease on everyone's part. Someone elected herself foreman; she barks orders while the rest of you scrub. She's over-the-top bossy.

Response: "No. I think doing it my way will be fairer and efficient. Let's try it."

Alert: People who take charge expect you to comply. Dispute them. Getting comfortable saying no sooner rather than later will help you navigate (and potentially avoid) future skirmishes.

••• SCENARIO •••

"Your website is so well done. It's exactly my style. Do mine?"

What's Going on Here: You took endless night classes to learn how to code. This person either doesn't realize or is ignoring how expensive the classes were and how much time it takes to build a website.

Response: "I wish it was that easy, but no."

Alert: Pay special attention when requests are huge and time-consuming.

··· SCENARIO ···

"Will you help me put this bookcase back together before my company arrives tomorrow? When I repair something, it looks ready to be carted to the dump. When you do it, it looks brand new."

What's Going on Here: Your friend flatters you to engage your skills. You haven't had this much praise since you mastered tying your shoelaces. It's your ego that wants to say yes to keep the compliments coming, but you've seen the bookcase—it will take more than a day to get it in shape. Rein in your ego before responding.

Response: "Thanks for the compliment. It's a big job, but you can do it. You underestimate your ability."

Alert: Be leery of those who call you an expert. Flattery can catch you off guard and get you to say yes pronto. Return a compliment with a compliment to build the other person's confidence.

··· SCENARIO ···

"Don't you think I should buy that condo (or new car or stock)?"

What's Going on Here: You're on shaky ground, particularly if you are not knowledgeable in that area. While you may think the proposed purchase is a good idea, your relationship could be strained if your advice is wrong—if the car turns out to be a lemon or the stock tanks, for example.

Response: "I don't know." Or, "I'm not comfortable giving my opinion when it's your money."

Alert: By backing off, you make it clear that you are not willing to give advice.

··· SCENARIO ···

"Will you show me how to use my 'new' laptop?"

What's Going on Here: You thought you were being a good guy; you gave your friend a "steal" on your old computer or other electronic equipment, and she thinks because you once owned it, you are responsible for its performance. Seemingly manageable requests have a way of escalating out of proportion into time-consuming commitments: phone calls with questions about lost files, malfunctioning Internet connections, viruses. All that can go wrong likely will, especially if you're dealing with someone who normally requires a lot of hand-holding.

Response: "No, I think you'll learn faster from a professional or someone more tech savvy than I am."

Alert: Be very specific about the amount of time you are willing to invest in someone else's computer literacy.

··· SCENARIO ···

*"You're stopping for something for
dinner, right? Just checking."*

What's Going on Here: It's a given: you are the one who drives fifteen minutes out of your way to pick up take-out when the person you live with drives right by the store.

Response: "No, you'll have to buy dinner tonight. Anything you like is fine with me." Or, "You know what I like." Or, "Get the usual."

Alert: Don't underestimate your partner's ability to handle chores routinely handled by you. If you're worried about his choices, give him a list, and praise his selections whatever he unpacks.

··· **SCENARIO** ···

"You need to get off that ridiculous diet.
This lobster-bacon macaroni and cheese is
delicious. A couple of bites won't hurt you."

What's Going on Here: You've spent hours at the gym sweating off pounds and are proud of your accomplishment. This person thinks the strict diet you've put yourself on is you fussing over nothing. Her initial bewilderment has turned into full-blown criticism and nagging.

Response: "Not a chance I am touching that. Looks good though."

Alert: Complying would make you feel awful and encourage her to keep ragging on you for working hard to stay in shape. Shouldn't she support and not undermine your efforts? Committing to a firm *no* is the best way to keep on track with your goals.

··· SCENARIO ···

*"Please text my date. Tell him I'm
sick and can't see him tonight."*

What's Going on Here: Your friend is in fine health but decided for whatever reason that she doesn't want to keep the date. You haven't told a successful lie in your life. It's not worth the shame you feel if you're caught.

Response: "No, I can't lie for you."

Alert: Never agree to do someone else's dirty work.

··· SCENARIO ···

*"If it's a boy, 'Max' is nice. And 'Madeline'
would be a beautiful name for a baby
girl—after Aunt Maddie?"*

What's Going on Here: Your parent or in-law is trying to engage you in a baby-naming session to find out what names you're considering (and to be sure you know what names she prefers). You are well aware of the family tradition of naming babies after people in one or both families and know your in-law or parent has high hopes you'll continue the tradition.

Response: "No. Probably not."

Alert: If you want to keep baby-naming between you and your partner, remind everyone that you need no help and will announce the baby's name when he or she is born.

··· **SCENARIO** ···

"Will you speak at George's funeral?"

What's Going on Here: It's an honor to be asked, but you have your doubts about standing up in front of a large crowd on such a sad occasion. You want to but are not sure you can eulogize George. Then again, how can you refuse?

Response: "No. I don't think I'm the right person; I'd be too emotional." Or, "I'm deeply moved that you asked me, but I'm afraid I have to say no." Or, "I can't speak to large groups." Or, "Have you asked Juan or Elise? They would be wonderful."

Alert: If you tense on hearing the request, no is the only answer that will spare you the anxiety you will surely feel on the day of the burial.

··· **SCENARIO** ···

"I'm going away next week. I know you love dogs. Will you take Jasper for the week?" a close friend asks. "He's not much trouble."

What's Going on Here: It's true, you love dogs, but you are intimidated by Jasper. He's big, tough, and not beyond skirmishes with other dogs. You are not sure you are strong enough to command him. You envision all kinds of problems cropping up, some not so pretty.

Response: "As much as I would like to help out, the fact is I don't think I can handle your dog. Let's think about someone else who can take him."

Alert: Whatever the situation, being honest about your fears or concerns as a reason for turning someone down is hard to argue with.

··· SCENARIO ···

"I know I ask for your help a lot.
Will you? It's important."

What's Going on Here: It could be a relative, friend, or coworker who wants something. You, being a people-pleaser, routinely agree, but you have decided enough is enough and are willing to risk his or her disappointment or a potential confrontation.

Response: "No, not this time."

Alert: A negative reaction to your *no* may suggest that your relationship hangs on your being agreeable and willing. It also may indicate that you are valued more for what you do for someone rather than for who you are.

··· 2 ···

With Friends

The very definition of friend makes saying no to one extremely difficult. Before deciding whether to deny a friend's request, make the distinction between who is a true friend and who is an acquaintance.

Social media networks govern much of our communication with and connection to friends. Friends we speak with every day as well as those we may not see in person for long swaths of time can reach out daily. You may come to feel closer to a friend and know a vast litany of details about his or her personal and professional life by scanning a social media page for updates, clicking through photos, or sending a message. With every lost connection from years ago rediscovered, new friend or long-term friend, friendships require reassessment from time to time.

Ask yourself: is this a friend with whom you have an equitable give-and-take, or someone who takes advantage of your good nature or availability? Friendships should be beneficial and satisfying to both parties. If you doubt a friendship is anything but genuine, a bit of food for thought: echoing the results of many studying friendship in recent years, MIT researchers found that around half the subjects who thought someone was a friend was not considered a friend in return.

Reevaluating your friendships doesn't mean you have to cut the cord with some; it can be a matter of figuring out on what level you want to interact. It can be great to meet for an occasional lunch or to attend sporting events, but working on the same committee or having daily interactions may be too much. Sometimes, taking a break from a friend is called for. Participating in activities together can bond two people, but if you feel more drained than invigorated, be mindful. If a friend who dreams of hiking the Appalachian Trail tries to pressure you—who hates being outdoors—into joining her, it may be time to step back. Not every friend has to be your closest or deserves your complete devotion. In the same vein, you will want to eliminate those who disappoint or let you down more often than not.

Seriously consider a smaller, more elite group of friends made up of those who truly care about and support you. When deciding who are acquaintances and who are real friends, know that science suggests solid friendships may help increase your lifespan. You have less of an option weeding out family members, but with friends you can be choosy.

Quiz: Are Your Friendships Balanced and Beneficial?

It may be time to shift your perception of certain friendships and how they operate. Paying attention to the questions you say yes to is a start:

1. Are you the person called when a friend needs a favor?
2. Do you spend most conversations with your friend listening to his or her problems rather than getting to speak about your own life?
3. Does most of what you and your friend do or talk about initially stem from his desires or concerns, not yours?
4. Do you know more about the drama at your friend's workplace in the last week than she does about the goings-on at your job?

5. Do you often find yourself agreeing with your friend to avoid conflict or tension?

6. Do some of your friends make you feel guilty? Has a friend purposely made you feel guilty more than once?

7. Have you put off hanging out with certain friends to prioritize the same ones over and over again?

8. Do you often leave a meeting with your friend feeling more emotionally drained than revitalized?

9. Do you sometimes dread meeting with your friend or wish you could do something else?

10. Do you "like" considerably more friends' Facebook or Instagram posts than they do of yours?

11. After being asked to do favors for your friends, do you suspect it wasn't because they admired your work, but because they didn't want to do them themselves?

12. Do you tend to agree with certain friends to avoid hurting their feelings?

A lot of yeses may indicate a friendship is a one-way street. This chapter offers ways to handle friendship fatigue, distance yourself from friends who force you into tasks you dislike, and reevaluate whether you may be looking for affection or approval from someone who may not belong in your core friendship circle.

Who's a Friend?

You depend on your friends, and they depend on you—perhaps in different ways than you thought, as your answers to the quiz may have revealed. One friend may act as your conscience or confidant; another as your cheerleader, your protector, or simply a good companion. Someone in your friend circle might nudge you to achieve more than you think you can. These friendships are valuable and positive, the ones that you want to preserve.

At the opposite end of the spectrum are negative friendships. To give you a sense of their impact, researchers found data to suggest that a poor friendship can have health implications equivalent to smoking fifteen cigarettes a day or drinking six alcoholic beverages a day. You may decide to take the drastic step of permanently severing a "friendship" that affects you negatively or ties to friends who contact you only when they want something.

Not everyone has to be your Best Friend Forever (your "BFF") or deserves your undivided attention. Saying no will not turn you into a bully or make you insensitive or petty. You won't stop helping others, but you'll become more discerning about how you respond and to whom.

Saying no to friends becomes simpler when you think about what's good for you and stop worrying about what someone else thinks. People have surprisingly short memories. Only you carry the weight and worry—topped with a few extra pounds of guilt. It's time to unload your conscience.

··· SCENARIO ···

*"Hey buddy, you don't mind being designated driver
again, right?" your friend texts you.
"You rock. Gas money on me!"*

What's Going on Here: This is the fifth time in a row you've been the designated driver for friends. You didn't mind at first.

Granted, you're not a huge drinker, but it would be nice to be the one to let loose once in a while. Your friend hasn't even thought to give you that option.

Response: "Nope, it's someone else's turn."

Alert: No amount of conciliatory gas money will replace a well-deserved night out. Be leery of friends who hope you go along with their plan.

··· SCENARIO ···

"Sorry we fell out of touch!" a friend e-mails you. "I'm back in town. Dinner tonight?"

What's Going on Here: You and Vivian used to be great friends, but your connection grew thin when she moved across the country. You fear losing touch altogether and are eager at a chance to rekindle—but tonight is short notice.

Response: "How about Saturday?"

Alert: When friends who were once very close are out of your day-to-day exchanges, they can become more like acquaintances and that can be troubling. You act friendly toward each other, but you know in your heart you aren't best of friends. You may want to jump at the opportunity to reestablish what you had, but take care to avoid changing plans you had with others or turning your schedule upside down.

··· SCENARIO ···

"U up?" your ex texts you as you're brushing your teeth before bed. "I need someone to talk to."

What's Going on Here: You both agreed to remain friends, and for a couple of months healthy boundaries stayed in place. But you've noticed your ex has fallen into old habits, turning to you for help with anything from work complaints to fights with his parents. At first, texting seemed to maintain more distance than seeing each other in person, but now it feels intrusive, like you can't get away from him.

Response: Ignore. Respond in the morning if you feel like it.

Alert: Text messaging is synonymous with twenty-first-century conversation. It's easier than ever to have an emotionally loaded back-and-forth. If you're starting to feel haunted by a friend's texts, not responding sends the strongest message that a line is being crossed.

··· **SCENARIO** ···

"The fabulous co-op I saw last week is barely out of my range. This is a lot to ask, but I'm in a bind. Will you consider co-signing a loan for me? You know I'm reliable."

What's Going on Here: Your friend is right. It *is* a lot to ask. Things get tangled when friends ask to borrow small amounts of money—co-signing can mess with your credit rating or even saddle you with 100 percent of the loan if your friend can't make payments.

Response: "I know how set you are on this dream home, but I can't."

Alert: This is not a one-time loan that a friend can easily repay. Worst-case scenario, you're in a financial nightmare, with only yourself to blame.

··· SCENARIO ···

*It's your third date, and halfway through
she/he wants to take a selfie. "What's
your user name? So I can tag you."*

What's Going on Here: It's been tricky enough trying to figure out if you'll remain friends or if the relationship is going anywhere. It doesn't seem like the greatest idea to take a picture and post it online. You can see the comments already: "Is this a new relationship?" "Who's the cutie?" "So I guess you're over Carlos now?"

Response: "I don't think I look great today. I don't mind taking a picture, but please don't post it."

Alert: Social media affects many aspects of dating. Some people may be more open than others to broadcasting their dating life. Your discomfort is valid. Change the subject, and change your date if the request is not honored.

··· SCENARIO ···

*Plans were made. Only when you're in the car and
on your way does your friend say, "Can we stop at
Sal's on our way back? It will only take a sec."*

What's Going on Here: Your friend throws her all-too-familiar curveball once she has you captive. She thinks she can add extra stops at a shoe store, a grocery, another friend's house, wherever, but she never tells you or asks you if you have the time or if you object until you are in her car. If you don't say something, you know that you will simmer the entire time you're together.

Response: "No, I have to be back by six. We can't do anything else or I will be too late for my sitter (an appointment, to start dinner)."

Alert: Listen for the "one more thing" ruse and don't allow it when it irritates you. You're not your friend's car service.

··· **SCENARIO** ···

*"I'm coming to town for a week, same week
as last year. Can I stay with you?"*

What's going on here: It's beginning to feel like you run a bed-and-breakfast for everyone who visits your city. You enjoy houseguests, but this particular person has worn out her welcome after six years. On top of being a world-class moocher, she reports the minutia of each day's events—boring! A few days you can handle, but a week is grating.

Response: "It would be nice to see you and catch up, but that's not going to be convenient."

Alert: Don't feel guilty about ending a freeloader's run, especially if it's been a long one. Chances are she'll focus on finding hospitality elsewhere and not on the fact that she can't stay with you. When she's worn out her welcome, you have every right to move her out of your friend circle.

· · · · · · · · · · · ·

Friendship Fatigue

Friendships have different levels of duration, depth, and responsibility. They continually evolve—or erode—because people change. Sometimes a friend who could be counted on expects too much or becomes overly dependent. Maybe this friend bombards you for advice or, contrarily, gives you too much advice. A friend can become too nosy, overly bossy, generally difficult, judgmental, or display all manner of annoying behavior that is tiresome and at times hard to take.

You want to be helpful, but when the friendship seems to be moving in a lopsided direction, you have to take a stand. Whether or not you understand a friend's motivation, saying no may be your only means of self-protection.

Saying no is often the route to retaining the friendships you hold dear, the ones that reflect the core elements that apply to meaningful friendships: concern and caring, support and trust, mutual respect, acceptance, respect of privacy, and the ability to listen.

··· SCENARIO ···

*"Can I borrow that cashmere thingy
you wore to Lana's party?"*

What's Going on Here: We're all taught to share. It's a virtue right up there with patience and cleanliness. If you lent items in the past, a friend will expect you to hand them over without a blink. If you say okay, you'll be watching her in your favorite sweater, worrying about the underarm stain she might leave or the spots she might add. You won't enjoy yourself.

Response: "I haven't decided what I'm wearing." You can also say, "I paid a fortune for that and I'm not lending it, not even to you."

Alert: Lending items precious to you is beyond the call of friendship. Sharing everything you own is not measurement of loyalty or a requirement.

··· SCENARIO ···

"It was fun running into you at the bowling lanes the other night. You and I should start a league (book club, race-training team) together."

What's Going on Here: It's one thing to see this friend now and then, but running a scheduled get-together holds no appeal, though you would like to join a bowling team one day. This person has a reputation for being irresponsible; it's likely you will be the one making all the phone calls and arrangements.

Response: "Great idea, but I can't commit. Maybe we can talk about it again in a few months."

Alert: Say no when you sense—or know—agreement will likely mean you will be fully in charge.

··· SCENARIO ···

"Don't you think Kevin and Tricia went overboard on their wedding (on decorating their new house, on having such an extravagant first birthday party for their child)?"

What's Going on Here: You've long been bugged by your loose-lipped friend. Warning bells should be going off in your head. Repeated questions like these are attempts to extract information from you to feed the gossip train. Innocently revealing what the flowers or the photographer, the house addition or new floor cost could be inflated or twisted and divulged back to Kevin and Tricia eventually.

Response: "I haven't thought about that."

Alert: In situations like this, play it safe by playing dumb.

··· SCENARIO ···

"Up for happy hour?" a high school friend you've reconnected with texts you for the third time this week.

What's Going on Here: You seem to be her only familiar face since she moved to town. You've met up with her many times, and you feel she's being clingy.

Response: Extract yourself by texting, "I can't tonight." Add a friendly emoji to indicate you mean no hard feelings.

Alert: Start to wonder if your friend is having issues meeting other people to hang out with or if she's using you as a crutch. It might be time for some space for you and for her to establish her own friendship base.

··· SCENARIO ···

"What do you want to do?" asks your friend. He was the one to propose hanging out in the first place, but now that you're together nothing comes to mind.

What's Going on Here: As usual, he asks for your input under the guise of generosity, but really he expects you to do the heavy lifting to come up with a fun plan. The last few times you hung out, you ended up being the one searching for activities online, calling restaurants for reservations, or texting other friends to ask what they were up to while your friend stared at his Twitter feed.

Response: "I have no ideas. Why don't you come up with a couple ideas and I'll choose."

Alert: Listen for questions that repeatedly put you in charge. If the pattern persists with no improvement, it might be time to insist on having concrete plans before meeting face-to-face.

··· SCENARIO ···

"Will you rearrange the cabinet for me? Be sure you put the glasses on the bottom shelf and the bowls where I can reach them."

What's Going on Here: A friend moved into a new apartment and is unpacking. You stopped by to say hello, but within minutes she's enlisted your help. From the start, the request has conditions. You're helping a finicky friend who will change your arrangement as soon as you're out the door.

Response: "No, it's better if you do this yourself; you know exactly how you want it."

Alert: Fastidious or perfectionist friends will manage to find something wrong with what you do or how you do it.

··· SCENARIO ···

"I'm too flustered to respond to my sister's nasty text. Can you write it for me?"

What's Going on Here: Your friend is having a feud and in the heat of the moment turns to you.

Response: "I'm not going to step in. I think you'll figure out what to say."

Alert: By adding more than your two cents, you entangle yourself in an issue your friend needs to resolve herself. Plus, they'll likely be on good terms again, and her sister may resent you for sticking your nose in their drama.

••• SCENARIO •••

"How come everything in my life is a mess?"
a close friend groans. She proceeds to tell you
all that went wrong for her that week, as she
did the week before and will the week after.

What's Going on Here: You've become her shoulder to cry on and delving into her sob story over and over leaves you depressed.

Response: "No negative talk tonight. We are going to focus on the positive and have fun."

Alert: Toxic relationships with someone spilling a steady diet of woes make the listener feel worse and potentially ruin the good feelings you have about the friendship. We falsely believe that venting makes us feel better, like opening a pressure valve, but it's a momentary relief at best.

••• SCENARIO •••

"You would look a lot younger if you colored
your hair. Have you thought about it?"

What's Going on Here: Your friend is giving you her point of view, one you may not agree with. You don't want to be bothered with the time-consuming maintenance once you begin coloring your hair, and you're not unhappy with the gray. Rather

37

than come back with a barb or show your annoyance for her implying you don't look good, be gentle. Your friend will get the hint that she's gone over the line.

Response: "Thanks for the suggestion, but I like the gray. Makes me look distinguished."

Alert: A friend will very likely back off when she realizes you don't appreciate her beauty tips.

··· **SCENARIO** ···

"I'm so excited our kids are going to the same high school! I think we should co-manage the girls' basketball team. It'll be like the olden days," your childhood friend says.

What's Going on Here: You've given her a chance but found that she irritates you. You have completely different points of view as adults than you did as kids. You have become very different people; you're a liberal and she's ultraconservative (or vice versa), and that's only one of the areas in which you disagree. You hang on to the relationship because of history—she knows your siblings and parents; you shared the same experiences in elementary and high school and were on a championship-winning team together. But that was then; this is now.

Response: "That's such a cool idea, but that commitment won't work with my schedule."

Alert: If you ask yourself, "Why am I meeting this person?" the friendship has likely burned itself out. Difficult as it may be, let it go.

··· SCENARIO ···

*"Should I wear a paper bag over
my head until it grows out?"*

What's Going on Here: You're in murky waters—if you say you love your friend's haircut when you don't, your friend may know you are not being truthful. To ease her obvious distress at having chopped off all but an inch of her hair, it's best to keep your answer light.

Response: Laugh appreciatively at her attempt to joke, then say, "No, no bag needed."

Alert: When it comes to the touchy area of physical appearance, respond cautiously to loaded questions. It's too easy to hurt someone who is unsure or may be feeling vulnerable.

··· SCENARIO ···

*"Gabe is more adorable every time I see him!" your
best friend squeals, bouncing your one-year-old on
her lap. "You have to give him a brother or sister."*

What's Going on Here: You and your partner both believe in keeping your only child a singleton. You know your friend, who has four children, thinks it's all talk. She brings up the topic every time you are together.

Response: "Nope, he'll stay an only child forever."

Alert: One-child families, once stigmatized, are increasing in number in countries all over the world. Yet, many families face pressure and judgment from those who believe otherwise. Keep reminding yourself that your decision is best for you, and see less of friends who think otherwise if their comments upset you.

••• SCENARIO •••

"You should really be on this new social media app," your friend tells you over lunch.

What's Going on Here: Your friend is obsessed with social media. She's come to love a trendy new app so much that whenever you text to see what's new, she answers with something along the lines of "So much! Follow me to see for yourself." The last thing you want is another downloaded app, but you fear you're losing touch with friends if you don't give in and join the app brigade.

Response: "I don't think I'll ever get around to it. We can easily stay in touch in other ways."

Alert: The ubiquitous nature of social media may make it seem like it's harder to say no to requests than it actually is. True friendships will outlast any social media trends.

••• SCENARIO •••

Writing a public post on your Facebook wall for all your followers to see, your friend links to an article pertaining to a private conversation you recently had. "Read this," she writes. It's an article on dealing with anxiety issues—something you assumed she would keep to herself.

What's Going on Here: Your friend could genuinely see herself as helping you, but you absolutely thought she'd have the sense to keep such a thing confidential.

Response: Delete the post. Say to her in person, "Thank you for trying to help, but what I told you was between us."

Alert: You have the right to expect a friend will keep personal confidences. Think about the strength of the relationship; if you learned you can't tell her anything personal, don't.

··· SCENARIO ···

"Tell everyone about your boyfriend's moving in. Give us the details," your friend urges. "You told me," she reminds you in front of everyone at the table.

What's Going on Here: You told your closest friend the intimate conversation you had with your boyfriend that led to the decision to live together. You are a private person and don't want to provide the romantic details to all the women gathered.

Response: "Yes, we will move in together in a few weeks when his lease is up. I am really happy. Let's leave it at that."

Alert: Because you "spilled the beans" to a close friend doesn't mean you have to share your personal life with acquaintances. Changing the subject or posing a question to someone else at the table moves the conversation away from you.

··· SCENARIO ···

"Break up with that guy, already." Your friend sternly advises you to ditch your most recent significant other.

What's Going on Here: Could be that your friend sees something troublesome that you can't or don't want to acknowledge. Could be that she honestly believes your partner "drags you down." Could be that your friend resents the time you spend doing couple activities, leaving less time for her. Carefully weigh if your friend is merely looking out for her own interests (having more of you) or if she may be jealous.

Response: "Thank you for trying to protect me."

Alert: Worry about the quality of friendship you have with people who selfishly try to be the architects of your love life. It is easy to advise others or for others to tell you what to do when they don't have to make the big decision.

··· SCENARIO ···

A friend you admire spouts an opinion you vehemently disagree with. "Aren't I right?" she asks.

What's Going on Here: You rarely contest this friend and have come to think if you disagree or argue, she will criticize you. Going along with her is more important than standing up for what you believe. You want her to like you as much as you like her.

Response: "I actually see that a bit differently."

Alert: Watching what you say to keep the relationship enjoyable or to gain approval can become nerve-wracking. If your opposing belief is enough for you to be soured in her eyes, perhaps you need a different friend.

··· SCENARIO ···

*"I'm ordering another drink. Should I get
you one, too?" your friend says, slurring
the words as he heads toward the bar.*

What's Going on Here: Your good friend has had too much to drink, and it isn't the first time. You think he needs to address his drinking, something you see as a problem.

Response: "No, thank you . . . and I feel strongly that you should call it a night as well."

Alert: No question you are venturing into volatile ground, but if you are a real friend, you will encourage your buddy to address his alcohol issues. He may be furious with you initially, but down the road, he is likely to thank you or at least appreciate your concern.

. . . .

You're Invited

It's affirming to be popular, to be included and wanted, to be swamped with invitations—to weddings, baby showers, bar and bat mitzvahs, and new house and dinner parties. Even if you attend everything you are invited to or want to, it may not be wise. While it's impressive to be available and adaptable, a strategic *no* helps avoid social burnout.

Granted, it's never easy to tell someone you can't attend his son's graduation luncheon or her mother's birthday bash when that occasion is of utmost importance to the host. For chronic people-pleasers, equally difficult are invitations to movies you don't want to see, trips you don't want to take, and get-togethers you may not be in the mood for. Here are predicaments and approaches you can try to ensure you accept only the invitations that are a priority to you.

··· SCENARIO ···

"Can we get together New Year's Eve?"

What's Going on Here: New Year's Eve carries a sense of urgency, a command performance—one in which you're supposed to be jolly and entertaining even if you don't feel like it. The pressure to celebrate is enormous and can leave you feeling confused about with whom you want to party or if you want to party at all.

Response: "No, we're staying home this year." Or, "It's too early to know what we want to do."

Alert: How you decide to celebrate a holiday needs no explanation. There will be plenty of other opportunities to see friends throughout the year.

··· SCENARIO ···

"We're having our annual Derby Day party. We're expecting you."

What's Going on Here: Horse racing holds no fascination for you. You'd rather clean a closet or read a book. However, you've gone every year and you're a little worried about how friends will perceive your backing out. Your friends are very sensitive, after all, and may feel insulted if you don't go. You can't say you're busy, because you knew the invitation was coming; it comes every year—and with it that dreaded sense of obligation.

Response: "I want to be with everyone, but I can seriously live without the Derby. Thank you, but I'm passing this year."

Alert: Beware of people who make assumptions or are so self-confident that they back you into a corner. You're entitled to your preferences and to act on them.

··· SCENARIO ···

"I signed you up for the ski trip the weekend of the twenty-fourth. We're going to have such a good time."

What's Going on Here: Most of us have a friend or two who micromanages other people's lives and, when given room, your life. Micromanagers possess finely honed skills to rope you in so subtly that you hardly realize what's happened. When someone runs your life or tries to, it can feel as if you're a pawn or as if he owns you. It may take a while to recognize the pattern; it will persist unless you derail him.

Response: "No, I know you may think I'm a lousy friend, but I don't want to go. Count me out." Or, "I made other plans that weekend, please take me off the list."

Alert: People who control others don't anticipate no for an answer. Even if you've been agreeing to a friend's directives for a long time, you can get free. Refuse once or twice and he will ask before obligating you again without your permission.

··· SCENARIO ···

"My sister's wedding is the tenth of next month. Don't make any other plans," the person you have been dating reminds you.

What's Going on Here: You want to end the relationship, and every time you start to walk away, he or she makes you an amazing dinner or finds the perfect chair for your apartment. The relationship is cozy, so you let it stroll along. You know in your heart it's going to end at some point because the chemistry is missing—at least on your end.

Response: "I'll try, but I'm not promising. I'm not sure I want to meet your family yet."

Alert: Going to family functions together, particularly significant ones, entangles you and sends a message of hope when you know differently. Sever the ties as soon as you can so it hurts less.

··· SCENARIO ···

"Bring salad. I've got everything else covered."

What's Going on Here: Kelley calls you at home after work to invite you to a small dinner party at her place this coming weekend. You're dog-tired. No way you want to be in charge of salad—there's too much prep time involved. When you're tired, your resistance is low and you're apt to agree. Think: What can I offer that is easy?

Response: "I'd rather not make salad. I'll bring wine."

Alert: It's okay to contribute in a way that works for you.

··· SCENARIO ···

*"We're planning a surprise party
for Jake. Will you come?"*

What's Going on Here: You're not close to Jake. Maybe you hardly like Jake. You could be shocked that you're on the invitation list because you and Jake had a major falling out ages ago and are not speaking. Clearly the person contacting you has no idea.

Response: A straightforward "No, thank you, wish I could join you" will get you out of a potentially awkward situation.

Alert: Don't discuss the details of the difficulties between you and Jake. It's probably the last thing the person calling cares to hear about.

··· SCENARIO ···

*"The craft show opens Friday night.
It's near my office. I'll meet you there after work."*

What's Going on Here: Dictatorial people are hard to refuse. They know what they want and when they want it and are not concerned if you are inconvenienced. And, not surprisingly, whatever it is almost always makes their life easier than it makes yours. You want to attend, but if you say yes to Friday night, you'll be driving miles in rush-hour traffic, and that doesn't make sense.

Response: "Friday is not good for me. Let's go first thing Saturday morning."

Alert: To make your life less difficult, present an alternative that suits you better. People who make the best arrangements for themselves are the ones who know what they want and say so.

··· SCENARIO ···

"We found you the perfect guy. Dinner at our place. Judd and I will be there to make the introduction easy and keep the conversation moving."

What's Going on Here: You've had more blind dates than you care to recall. None of them, particularly the ones that Farah and Judd arranged, were remotely interesting to you. They believe they are doing you a favor, but you already know the routine: another awkward, uncomfortable evening that can't end soon enough.

Response: "No, thank you. It's sweet of you to worry about me, but I'm taking a break from blind dates."

Alert: Because people care about you doesn't mean they understand what you want in a partner. Most likely good friends will not abandon you as a friend because you turn down their date "finds." They'll keep looking.

··· SCENARIO ···

"Are you going to Timothy Kerber's funeral?"

What's Going on Here: Everyone wants to do the right thing. Whoever asks is not necessarily trying to make you feel guilty. He may be deciding what to do based on what you plan.

Response: "No. I didn't know him very well, and I don't know anyone in his family." Or, "I'll go to the wake, but I'm not going to the funeral."

Alert: You don't have to go to a funeral because someone asks you if you'll be there, nor should you feel compelled to do so.

··· SCENARIO ···

"Let's go to Andre's Continental for dinner."

What's Going on Here: Andre's is one of the most expensive restaurants in the area, and you don't want to spend the money—or really can't afford to. Face it: you won't enjoy one bite because the price will be all you can think about. On the other hand, your style is to be obliging, and you don't want to appear cheap.

Response: "No, let's go somewhere less expensive."

Alert: Accept that you can't afford what your friend can. People are not mind readers. You can let them know you object without having an awkward argument or discussion. Doing so makes them more likely to understand and be considerate in their choices.

··· SCENARIO ···

*"You have to host the Super Bowl party.
You've done it for years. It's tradition."*

What's Going on Here: For what seems like a decade, your friends have gathered at your house to scream at the television set, drink your booze, and eat your food. The mess they leave behind is, well, a mess. Your enthusiasm has been on the wane for a long time, but you haven't wanted to disappoint them. You are tired of putting on your happy hostess face, wishing the fourth quarter would end.

Response: "No, I'm not hosting Super Bowl this year."

Alert: When you know the drill, don't let history repeat itself. Bowing out will enable someone who feels strongly about preserving a long-standing tradition to take over.

··· SCENARIO ···

*"What do you mean, you're not coming
to the picnic? Of course you are."*

What's Going on Here: Your friend loves picnics, and if she thought about it, she would remember that you don't. You can't be in the sun, don't like sand in your sandwich or pine needles in your potato salad. So what if she thinks you're the proverbial stick-in-the-mud? You'll be in an air-conditioned room relaxing over your meal and using the time to catch up on things you never get to.

Response: "No, I don't eat outdoors; you know that."

Alert: It may be time to reevaluate your friendships with those who don't remember your likes and dislikes or consider your comfort. Don't be bullied into being somewhere you don't want to be—in this instance, swatting flies and fending off mosquitoes. The itching isn't worth it.

··· SCENARIO ···

A mutual friend of Frank's, your dear friend who passed away, invites you to a public Facebook group. "Please share your memories of Frank."

What's Going on Here: Many immediately write adoring, flattering posts about Frank, and you start to feel that it looks odd that you, one of his closest friends, aren't sharing.

Response: Privately message the friend who started the Facebook group: "Thank you for doing this for Frank. I'm afraid I'm not ready to share."

Alert: Not being comfortable enough to share online is perfectly normal. People grieve differently—some publicly, others privately. It's unlikely your friend or others will judge you for not posting your thoughts.

··· SCENARIO ···

"Let's hit the mall on Saturday."

What's Going on Here: You love this friend dearly and have lots in common, but not shopping styles. You know what you want, find it fast, and buy it. She touches every garment in the store, tries on half of them, then agonizes over whether to spend the money. Usually, she doesn't.

Response: Tell her the truth: "You and I can't shop together; you drive me nuts." Or, "Our shopping strategies are so different. Let's grab lunch instead."

Alert: Shopping with someone whose speed and approach don't match yours promises to be a long, excruciating process, one you surely want to skip.

••• **SCENARIO** •••

"I have two tickets for the opening of the new play at Graham-Bell Theatre for tomorrow night."

What's Going on Here: It's pretty straightforward: you're invited to attend a play. The hitch: you don't like the subject matter, heavy drama, or either of the leads.

Response: "Thank you, it was so thoughtful of you to invite me. I really prefer musicals. Maybe Ali or Seth or Daniel want to go; they enjoy dark drama."

Alert: You don't have to like everything friends like to keep them in your circle or to be in theirs.

• • • • • • • • • • • •

Out and About: Social Graces

The desire to say no briskly vanishes under the pressure of social protocols. Unspoken rules and expectations of what good friends do can lead you to say yes to things that you don't want to do but feel you must. You wind up saying yes simply to be gracious.

Being socially correct about perceived obligations gets dicey, especially if you pride yourself on being polite and "correct." You may believe you are committing a social no-no when you refuse an invitation or refrain from responding to online messages or requests. Pinpointing smart ways to extricate yourself—yet remain courteous and in the good graces of friends and acquaintances—is a powerful way to stand up for yourself.

··· SCENARIO ···

"We're holding a garage sale in two weeks. Will you help me set up and keep me company?"

What's Going on Here: You're wanted—and needed—for your keen ability to organize as well as for your companionship. Your friend will have you at her house days in advance, sorting, pricing, setting up card tables, and telling her what she needs to do in the way of advertising. You'll be enlisted to post signs and make lunch. Her garage sale could consume four or more days of your time.

Response: "I have all day Friday to get you ready, but I can't be there on sale day."

Alert: Be discerning in how you offer your time. Do what you can to have the event run smoothly, but clearly define the amount of time you offer.

··· SCENARIO ···

"You unfollowed me on Twitter. Are you serious? Is it a mistake?" an acquaintance asks pointedly the next time you see him in person.

What's Going on Here: You find this person's tweets to be utterly nonsensical, plus the sheer volume constantly clutters your feed. You know you're probably not the first friend to unfollow but haven't heard of him accusing others. You're also surprised that he apparently combs through his followers list enough to notice your absence.

Response: "Please don't take it personally. I'm streamlining my account."

Alert: It's unfortunate when someone's tweets aren't your cup of tea, but you're not responsible for his feelings. No need to disparage his Twitter account, but no need to re-follow, either.

··· SCENARIO ···

You get a notification on the new dating app you've been using: "Can we meet?"

What's Going on Here: You've searched a few of the dating service profiles and at last found a potential date. You've seen his picture and he's more than passable. You've exchanged a steady stream of chats, and now he wants a face-to-face. And yes, you led him on a bit in an effort to get the ball rolling, but a couple things he wrote set off your inner alarm.

Response: "No, I don't think it's a good idea." Or, don't respond. If his persistence bothers you, block his messages or his profile.

Alert: Don't worry about hurting the feelings of someone you don't really know. Missed connections and fizzled threads happen all the time. Don't fret over any supposed obligations to take the next step. Listen to your inner voice and protect your time. Swipe to the next photo.

··· SCENARIO ···

"Check out the guy with the blond hair over by the bar; he's adorable and looking right at you—an invitation if I ever saw one. Go talk to him."

What's Going on Here: Your friends coax you; they resort to name-calling, referring to you as a coward and a wimp. They are on your case and wearing you down. You think you should start a conversation with the guy simply to shut them up.

Response: "If he wants to talk to me, he knows where I am."

Alert: Don't let people goad you into doing things that you feel are chancy, that compromise who you are, or that you'll dislike yourself for doing.

··· SCENARIO ···

"Did you get my link to donate to my project's Kickstarter page???" a friend messages you on Facebook the moment you go online. "You're going to donate, yes?"

What's Going on Here: You are not particularly close with this friend, but he bombards you with e-mails, posts, texts, and messages concerning raising money for his latest venture. You have no interest in or passion for this project but don't want to come off as cold-hearted or impolite.

Response: "I'm not in a position to donate to your project right now, but I wish you the best of luck."

Alert: You can't seem to escape news of a friend's project, but you are not obligated to give your money to a cause you don't believe in—especially if you know you'll be annoyed or feel defeated if you give in.

··· SCENARIO ···

*"I got a job offer. The move would be
lateral, a little more money, but a change.
The new job has some distinct opportunities
for promotion, but I like where I am."*

What's Going on Here: It feels like a question, but it isn't. Don't assume your friend is looking to you for a solution when he or she makes a statement. Wait for a question that asks for your help: "What do you think I should do?" for example.

Response: "Talk to me about the pros and cons of the offer."

Alert: Avoid giving advice unless you are directly asked. If you take the "bait" and essentially answer a question that wasn't asked, you wind up giving unsolicited advice, possibly where none was wanted or warranted.

··· SCENARIO ···

*An e-mail arrives in the middle of your workday.
A friend has posted a glowing endorsement on your
LinkedIn page and invites you to do the same.*

What's Going on Here: You were both happy to collaborate as consultants on a project with a third friend awhile back. You are surprised at how kind his testimonial is. You want to take time to write something and are afraid that if you don't do it now, it'll fall by the wayside.

Response: "Thank you!" in a return e-mail. Then write short notes to yourself on what you might say and make time later in the day to refine your testimonial.

Alert: It may feel urgent to drop everything and comply with his request, since he was especially nice to you. Ignore the pressure to return the favor instantly. You'll do a better job if you take time to think it through.

··· SCENARIO ···

"Will you pick the restaurant for Saturday night?"

What's Going on Here: Your friends want to leave the dining decision to you. That would be fine if every time you chose a restaurant they didn't find fault with the food, the service, the prices, the ambiance, or the noise level. While there's a lot to like about this couple, dining with them has become tedious. Have your answer ready.

Response: "No, thanks. You choose; you know what we like."

Alert: With impossible-to-please friends, bow out of making choices so you don't have to listen to them complain.

··· SCENARIO ···

You both saw the waiter put the check dead in the middle of the table. She's not making any move to pick it up, and you don't want to.

What's Going on Here: You consider yourself a generous person, but you repeatedly get stuck with the tab when the two of you eat together. You don't remind your friend how much she owes you because talking about money embarrasses you. You don't want to make a fuss but have been pushed into paying more than you should in the past and would be very unhappy if it happened again.

Response: "I dislike talking about money, but I can't treat you every single time. I have to watch what I spend, too. I'll pay tonight, but we have to have an agreement. We'll split checks from now on."

Alert: The fact that your friend never has cash or is maxed out on her credit cards is not your problem. If questioned, state plainly what you think is fair. If and when you go out again, remind her that you agreed to split the bills, if you did. She's been forewarned and will be ready for your *no*.

··· SCENARIO ···

"Hey friend!" a text from an unfamiliar number reads. "I'm so happy you're interested in jogging together. I typically start at 5:30 a.m. Meet you at . . . ?"

What's Going on Here: You remember that you passed your number to this new acquaintance when you met at the grocery store. She actually followed up on your casual remark that you'd like to start running. You definitely don't want to wake at dawn and exercise with someone likely levels above you, but now the text is sitting there in your phone. She took the time to invite you—it's only polite to agree and give it a shot, right?

Response: "That time really doesn't work for me, unfortunately." Or, "To be honest, I've thought about it and I think another workout routine is more my style." Or, "Thanks for the offer, but I'll pass this time."

Alert: Consider the text a kind gesture, not an obligation. If she takes your response as a rebuff, it's probably best to maintain distance anyway and be pleasant if you run into each other.

··· SCENARIO ···

"If we go to the jazz festival this weekend, I'll go anywhere you want to go next weekend. Deal?"

What's Going on Here: This is enticing because you know exactly what you want to do next time. However, if you made similar deals with this friend in the past and he doesn't hold up his end of the bargain, think again.

Response: "No deal."

Alert: Be wary of friends who barter for your time; everyone may not be as good to his word as you are.

··· SCENARIO ···

"I'm lending my car to my brother while we're away next week. Can I borrow Alex for a few hours on Saturday to follow me to his house and bring me back?"

What's Going on Here: Friends regularly ask permission to "borrow" your partner, be it to help move a couch, fix their garage doors, find a leak . . . He's strong, handy, and agreeable. You know it's over an hour-and-a-half drive one way to her brother's house. He'll be gone four or five hours minimum.

Response: "I really need Alex on Saturday." You could add the truth: to hang the blinds; to take the dog to the vet; to babysit while I have a birthday lunch with my sister.

Alert: Be selfish about lending your best helper when you may need him yourself.

··· SCENARIO ···

"I'll be in Chicago for a few days, so we will have lots of time to catch up."

What's Going on Here: You want to see your friend, but you know she expects you to clear your calendar for her. She's possessive and self-centered. If you don't have every minute when you're not at work to devote to her, she plays the guilt card by saying, "Oh, I thought you'd be excited to see me."

Response: "That week is really crammed with dates. I won't be able to be with you full-time, but we'll still see each other."

Alert: Don't stop your busy life and allow a friend to monopolize it during an occasional visit. Include her in plans where you can.

··· SCENARIO ···

"The Goodmans had a baby yesterday. Can you make a meal and bring it over sometime this week?"

What's Going on Here: Your church or your friend group expects its members to provide meals for people who have had a significant event in their lives—a new baby, an illness, a death. Helping now and again makes you feel you are giving back. You want to cook for the Goodmans, but right now you don't have time to shop for the ingredients, prepare a meal, and deliver it.

Response: "Can't this week, but try me another time. I always want to help out when I can."

Alert: Don't overextend yourself or else volunteering will become a chore that you won't feel like doing.

· · · · · · · · · · ·

In the Neighborhood

For most of us, neighbors are people with whom we would like to maintain polite, civil relationships. The close proximity leads to essential give-and-take. These relationships are also open season for a friend or neighbor taking advantage of your readiness to be there. All of a sudden, you find yourself assuming annoying or time-consuming responsibilities solely to be neighborly.

Keeping neighbor-to-neighbor relations amicable can be challenging and tricky, yet putting off refusals is the same as having threatening storm clouds over your head. When possible, firmly rejecting a request at the onset is usually the better option and permits everyone to carry on with or without your help.

··· SCENARIO ···

"You have to join the neighborhood Facebook group," the woman down the street implores. "We're organizing together to keep everyone informed of neighborhood news."

What's Going on Here: Your neighbor believes that everyone would benefit from this Facebook page. You barely enjoy face time with your neighbors in the real world—you keep to yourself and don't want to connect on social media.

Response: "I'm hardly ever on my own Facebook page. Is there a bulletin board at the community center I can keep an eye on?"

Alert: Given most everyone's addiction to social media, when you don't respond to posts or add anything to the conversations, member reaction to your Facebook "silence" might be more negative than if your name isn't on the list in the first place. Similarly, joining and subsequently opting out may draw unwanted attention.

··· SCENARIO ···

"Can you drive carpool for me?"

What's Going on Here: The scheduled driver offers no hint of a possible emergency or suggestion that you would be doing her a favor. She's done this before. It's not your day to chauffeur, and you've made other plans. If you don't drive, you're concerned that the children will miss the soccer game. Don't be so sure. It is not your responsibility to see that they get to every soccer game. When you say no, in all likelihood, the other parent will find a way to get her child and yours to the game.

Response: "No, I have plans."

Alert: If you willingly fill in this time, move yourself to the "sucker" category and count on being asked again and again.

··· SCENARIO ···

"The older boys who keep taking over the park playground need to be kicked out," your neighbor writes in a massive e-mail thread. "Respond if you're on the side of safety."

What's Going on Here: You signed up for what you thought was a neighborhood watch newsletter and soon realized that the administrator who lives three houses down broadcasts a litany of angry complaints. The last few e-blasts have felt more like aggressive diatribes than informative safety measures.

Response: Nothing. Or, block the chain or unsubscribe.

Alert: The urge to join forces "if you're on the side of safety" is a pressuring tactic. Chances are you're not the only one who feels perturbed.

··· SCENARIO ···

Mrs. Locke, your elderly neighbor, lives alone and recently recovered from surgery. She calls to ask if you would buy a birthday card for her to send to her son.

What's Going on Here: Several months ago you told her son, who lives across the country, not to worry—you would do his mother's shopping, take care of her garbage and recycling, and check on her until she was back on her feet. You did that, and more. You cooked and brought her meals and drove her on errands long after she was able to drive again and manage her day-to-day needs herself.

Response: "Mrs. Locke, I can't get to the card store today. Why don't you pick up a card tomorrow when you're out shopping?"

Alert: After an emergency, when the person you are assisting can and should be independent again, you are doing her a disservice by prolonging the dependency. It's time to put *no* into action.

··· SCENARIO ···

"We need two hundred names on this petition,"
a neighbor says. He rambles on about what a
good thing the petition is for the community and
how everyone is signing. "Please, sign here," he
adds, thrusting a clipboard into your hand.

What's Going on Here: You're unclear on the issue or the group behind it. You don't know how the petition will be used and are therefore reluctant to sign on the spot.

Response: "I don't put my name on anything I haven't read thoroughly. Leave me a copy; I can't read it now."

Alert: Don't sign petitions of any type to get the person off your doorstep.

··· SCENARIO ···

*"Will you watch my child for an hour
on Thursday afternoon?"*

What's Going on Here: This isn't the first time your neighbor has asked. What's most irksome is that her idea of an hour is almost always protracted. She'll call to tell you she's stuck and apologize profusely—or she doesn't bother to call and you wait, watching for her car to pull into your driveway.

Response: "No, I can't on Thursday."

Alert: Watch for behavior in others that leaves you frustrated. When the sharing of child responsibilities isn't reciprocal, start asking for equal time instead of feeling used.

··· SCENARIO ···

A fellow PTA member complains about the all-school science fair assignment due Monday. "I'm practically illiterate when it comes to that stuff," she says. "Any ideas for Emmy?"

What's Going on Here: Whether or not he knows you excelled in the sciences and can think of twelve possible projects for you and his child to do together, you'd really rather not tie up your weekend. Refrain from saying, "I'd be glad to help."

Response: "I'll give your daughter a few suggestions, but I can't work with her this weekend."

Alert: You are still a good friend without sharing your talents with his children. It's enough that you are called on to craft magnificent solar systems and working rockets for your own offspring.

··· SCENARIO ···

*"Will you let the deliverymen into my house
sometime between noon and five? You
work from home; you'll be around."*

What's Going on Here: In spite of the incredible number of people who conduct business from their homes, the common belief is that those with home offices have the time to oblige their neighbors, friends, and family.

Response: "I'll be waiting for an important call." Or, "I have to run some business errands." Or, "I have a conference call scheduled." Or, "I'm on a deadline." In short, tell the neighbor it's impossible for you to watch for deliverymen for hours on a workday. It's disruptive enough when you have to do it for yourself.

Alert: To stop people from thinking you spend Monday through Friday staring into space, be unavailable to chat in the middle of the day. Draw boundaries by only answering work-related calls.

··· SCENARIO ···

*"Will you write a recommendation
to your college for my son?"*

What's Going on Here: You've been an interviewer for your alma mater for years, and you know your neighbor's child is not a candidate the college seeks. Your friend believes your recommendation counts, that it will wow admissions and get his son a spot in the freshman class.

Response: "My letter won't help. Admissions offices don't pay as much attention to alumni recommendations as they used to."

Alert: You've told the truth. Implying that you don't have much clout also makes the point that you aren't enthusiastic about recommending his child. You've said no indirectly and haven't compromised your integrity with the college.

••• SCENARIO •••

"Hope you don't mind, but they're coming to cut down our dead tree at eight on Saturday morning."

What's Going on Here: Your neighbor would not be asking if he were sure the time was okay. He knows you sleep late on Saturday. Most people say, "Fine. Thanks for letting me know," then fume about being woken up so early.

Response: "That's too early. Please ask them to start at nine."

Alert: Instead of accepting what people tell you, ask for a change.

••• SCENARIO •••

Your neighbor texts out of the blue: "I miss our walks. Can we start again next week?" It's the first you've heard from her in months.

What's Going on Here: A nasty argument over your shrubs, her dog, or the kids trampling her flowers a while back deeply affected the bond you used to have with this neighbor. Making amends feels like the proper thing to do, but she hurt you deeply with her vengeful words. You don't want to open yourself up again to that kind of abuse.

Response: "My schedule is packed. Let's touch base in a few weeks."

Alert: Some friendships don't bounce back completely from major conflicts. Whether you need time to assess your own vulnerability and reconnect at a later date or the relationship is something to walk away from entirely, preserve your right to maintain space.

··· SCENARIO ···

A child from the neighborhood dressed in her Girl Scout uniform rings your doorbell. "Hi, Mrs. D'Angelo, I'm selling cookies for my scout troop. Will you buy some?" Her mother stands in the background watching your reaction.

What's Going on Here: Cookies, candy, or another magazine subscription is not on your must-have list, but you want to be neighborly.

Response: "I placed an order with my niece" (if true). You could say, "I can't do it now (or today)" and hope she forgets to stop by another day.

Alert: It's nearly impossible to refuse a child you know. However, you can say no to children you don't know and should turn away anyone raising money for causes that are unfamiliar or could be scams.

··· SCENARIO ···

*"Will you request my son Michael for the
team you're coaching this season?"*

What's Going on Here: Your neighbor is asking you to use your
influence as a coach with the "powers" that make up the
town's sports teams.

Response: "Michael's so good, he will do well on any team. He's
got real potential."

Alert: You've taken an approach that will hopefully move your
friend's focus back where it should be: on his son's athletic
prowess. Without saying so, you've refused and not been
forced to make a request that's potentially awkward when the
coaches sit down to assign players to teams.

··· 3 ···

All in the Family

For most of us, family is foremost. Because family members tend to feel closer at hand than friends and colleagues, we want to keep friction low, camaraderie high. Family is our support system, often our cheerleaders. In the best of all worlds, its members—parents, in-laws, sisters, brothers, cousins—are the people we turn to in good times and bad. We depend on them possibly more than we depend on friends. Yet, these very same relatives take advantage if given the opportunity.

Many worry that saying no to family paints them as disinterested or uncaring. There is a difference between making noble sacrifices to get things done for the good of the family (or one relative in particular) and being seen as the family softy.

Refusing can get sticky. One seemingly innocuous *no* can ignite a family feud or division that lasts for months, years, or a lifetime. While it's feasible to dismiss a friend in order to make life less chaotic, it's harder to ignore a relative. Technology ups the stakes: Family requests are potentially more frequent and social media interaction unavoidable. Relatives have immediate access to you, testing your boundaries.

Take the quiz below to help determine if you are the point yes-person within your family—the one who regularly gives in to requests and handles most problems.

Quiz: Are You the Yes-Person in Your Family?

If you have more *yes* than *no* answers, it may be time to forge new or stronger family boundaries.

1. Do you find yourself often taking up extra tasks because no one else will?
2. Do you often agree to attend family events even when you don't want to go? Do you feel you can't ignore or change family traditions?
3. Do you think you have no choice in following family members on social media, in spite of the fact that what they post often upsets you?
4. Have you been roped into a family text thread, writing something when you don't want to be part of the conversation?
5. When hosting family gatherings, do you make a main course . . . and a vegan dish for your niece Andrea . . . and a nut-free dessert for Uncle Simon . . . *and* a side of plain mashed potatoes for your picky nephew or grandson?
6. Are you frequently the designated peacemaker in family disputes?
7. When relatives gather in your home, do you find yourself surrounded by people on their smartphones and don't ask them to put them away?
8. When family is together, do you laugh at or ignore a relative's jokes made at your expense?
9. Does a sibling or other relative forward you countless e-mails that you have no interest in? (Have you asked him or her to stop?)
10. Are you the preferred family member to turn to when someone can't figure out how to upload photos or has new software to be installed?

11. Do you follow an elder's—your mother's or mother-in-law's—instructions and do it "her way" to avoid reprimand or upsetting her?

As enjoyable as relatives can be, there are times they invade your privacy, ask the outrageous, or make demands that as a busy adult you can't meet. Remember: in the same way that bending backward for what friends ask doesn't strengthen a friendship, bending to accommodate family doesn't make you a better relative. But because of the history, close ties, and traditions, saying no seems impossible. To make it harder, relatives are much more likely to know your weaknesses, and when they hone in on one, your resistance evaporates.

You are not responsible for relatives' happiness or comfort. One person can't do or be everything for everyone in the family. That alone should reduce your stress level when you find yourself in situations that call for a *no*. In this chapter, anecdotes provide specific paths forward.

Parent and In-Law Traps

Parents present the supreme challenge in the quest to mark boundaries and be more of a no-person. Perhaps both parents, or one more so than the other, spent their parenting careers getting you to be polite and obedient, to do what they said when they said it. Over the years you have developed set patterns of reacting to your parents' requests. But times have changed. You are a grown-up with a life and perhaps a family of your own.

You no longer have to be the amenable, compliant child. You will be much happier when you get out from under a parent's annoying or even domineering demands. Yet many adult children fearing tension or conflict have trouble realizing the fact that they can turn down a parent's request or command.

Few adult children set out to insult, hurt, or disregard their parents. But, there may be many times when parents continue to advise, protect, and think they know what's best. You may believe that, because your parent asks, saying yes is mandatory, that shaking your head no is unthinkable. Even if they're towns or states away, it can feel as if your parents live next door—that your yeses are expected.

It's no secret that many of us encounter similar feelings with in-laws. The joining of families brings in-laws plenty of unknown terrain to navigate. Until you came on the scene, they pretty much ran the family their way; they had more attention from their son or daughter, and while they may adore you (or say they do), you pose a barrier. A son- or daughter-in-law represents changes they may not appreciate or like. Given these realities, in-laws, like parents, can unsettle your grown-up life or make it difficult—when you allow it.

Many times with parents and in-laws you can anticipate situations and problems. In those cases, picture yourself saying no as a means to buttress your courage. Saying no when you need to, even if parents or in-laws are not consistently intrusive, will help validate your independence and force them to realize you have "graduated" to a life that is neither totally dependent on them nor revolves around them. After a few nos, their expectations will change.

Note: You can substitute "parents" for "in-laws" or vice versa in numerous situations.

··· SCENARIO ···

"I need you at the house to help your father with . . ."

What's Going on Here: Your parent thinks she can tell you what to do and you'll do it. You know that if you comply, you'll end up getting roped into twenty other tasks when you're there.

Response: "I'd love to help, but I can't do what you're asking."

Alert: Be careful not to revert back to your ten-year-old dutiful son or submissive daughter role. Be helpful when you can, but be sure the circumstances fit your schedule and willingness or you will be irritated by what a parent asks of you.

··· SCENARIO ···

"When are you going to change your maiden name on social media?" your new mother-in-law asks the next time she sees you.

What's Going on Here: You've long planned to change your name legally but keep it the same online for professional reasons. You've mentioned this once or twice, but clearly the message wasn't understood.

Response: "You know I love your son and your family, but changing my name would be confusing to work colleagues." Or: "It's important to keep my name consistent for work."

Alert: Deciding to change your name or not is a choice that is yours alone.

··· SCENARIO ···

"Book the flights for your mother and me?" your father asks, forwarding you an airfare deal he got in his inbox.

What's Going on Here: You thought you were being helpful when you showed your parents how to sign up for travel deal alerts, but they took that as a cue that you're their travel agent.

Response: "I'm sure you and Mom can figure it out. Call me if you get stuck."

Alert: Continuing to say yes to parents who are used to your dropping everything to help—be it booking flights, straightening out an online order, or coming to their rescue in some other way—only encourages them to lean on you more.

··· SCENARIO ···

"Wow, those are what your window treatments look like?" your mother says over FaceTime. She's glanced at the windows behind you and doesn't approve. "You need better-quality shades. I'll order ones that match the couch I got you."

What's Going on Here: Your mother hates that you live thousands of miles apart and shows her support by decorating your apartment from afar. Her concern has turned to head-on butting in. Your closet is full of items she's sent that aren't to your taste.

Response: "Thanks for the support, Mom, but I don't want new curtains. The windows are fine the way they are."

Alert: It makes your mom feel better to buy you things, but you're the one who has to live with the clutter. Cushion your response with thanks, but be firm that you do not want—or have room for—anything else.

··· SCENARIO ···

*"I haven't seen you in so long I
forget what you look like."*

What's Going on Here: Ah, manipulation in its purest form. The ploy is designed to elicit your guilt, especially if you have been ignoring your parent because your life is busy. Chances are a parent is likely to be as dismayed if you rush in and out as he would be had you not stopped in at all.

Response: "No, I love you and want to be with you. Let's set a date."

Alert: Put aside any inclination to make excuses. You are entitled to a life that excludes parents, in-laws, and other family some of the time.

··· SCENARIO ···

*"Hope it fits!" your father-in-law says as he
tosses a Los Angeles Dodgers hat your way.*

What's Going on Here: You are an ardent San Francisco Giants fan. You have no desire to own such a hat but don't want to be rude turning down a gift. You also don't want to create tension that could last years by responding in the wrong way.

Response: "Thank you, but I already have a hat to wear." Or, "I'll wear yours if you wear my Giants cap—but I have a feeling you won't want to."

Alert: A polite or playful response can offset a potential argument between passionate sports fans.

··· SCENARIO ···

"THIS is how you dress????" your mother publicly comments on a photo you posted on Facebook.

What's Going on Here: You saw no harm in accepting her friend request, but the judgmental comments she made when you were a teen have bled into your adult life online. You are afraid to start a back-and-forth drama, but you are seething.

Response: Tell her privately, "Mom, if you put comments like that on Facebook again, I will have to block you. It makes it seem as if I am still a little girl."

Alert: You are permitted to set online boundaries. Be prepared for your parent to be surprised, but it's important to send the message that you won't allow her to censure you in public. Seriously consider if your parent should have access to your Facebook page postings.

··· SCENARIO ···

"Try this!" your father says, placing a spoon of beef stew in front of your face. "I know it's your favorite."

What's Going on Here: Dad's beef stew was a favorite dish when you were a little kid, but your parents forget you're a vegan now. You get that he's trying to connect, but you bristle when he ignores your life choices.

Response: "It smells delicious, Dad. I can't. You must have forgotten that I don't eat meat."

Alert: A nudging request from your father can have a gentle response. You can say a clear "No, thanks," while reminiscing with him about eating the recipe on cold winter days years ago.

··· SCENARIO ···

*"I'm adding Aunt Becky and Uncle
Al to the wedding guest list."*

What's Going on Here: Aunt Becky is your mother's third cousin. You haven't seen her or Uncle Al since you were three years old, and you don't care to see them on your wedding day. You may have to remind your mother that this is *your* wedding, not the one she wanted for herself or dreamed of for you. She might argue and tell you that she and your father are footing the bill, but you still don't have to invite people you barely know to a celebration that is purportedly for you. Stand firm! Your parents will get the message.

Response: "No. I realize you don't want to hurt anyone's feelings, but we're trying to keep the wedding small. If we invite Aunt Becky, we have to invite her brothers and sisters, and on it goes. We'll be way over the number we agreed on."

Alert: You probably spent your life trying to please your parents, but you really can edit your wedding guest list.

··· SCENARIO ···

*Your husband answers the phone and says to
you, "Honey, it's your mother. Can you talk?"*

What's Going on Here: You spoke to your mother earlier in the day, and you can tell your husband knows it by the roll of his eyes. She's so sensitive that she's going to be hurt if you don't pick up the phone.

Response: "Tell her I'll call back later."

Alert: You don't have to be available to a parent constantly. Whatever your mother has to say probably can wait. It's a good idea to arrange set times to talk, so you don't have to avoid her calls.

••• SCENARIO •••

"We're giving all the children the new iPad as their holiday gift this year," your parents or in-laws announce.

What's Going on Here: Grandparents tend to be generous and sometimes excessive with grandchildren. You are trying to teach a respect for and an understanding of money. Extravagant gifts don't help your mission.

Response: "That's a lovely idea, but you need to wait a year or two. We don't think they are old enough, and Helena, while the oldest, loses everything."

Alert: Well-meaning grandparents (or other relatives) can undo your progress in instilling the values you hold high. You can be diplomatic in your refusal by being appreciative of the suggestion.

••• SCENARIO •••

"Do you mind if I bring Sandra with me when I come to visit next weekend?"

What's Going on Here: Sandra is your mother's best friend and constant sidekick since your parents' divorce. Sandra is hypercritical and takes over your home the second she arrives. You rarely say no to your mother and are afraid to start now, but you don't want to be bothered by Sandra's meddling ways.

Response: "Mother, no, I prefer you came alone. We don't need Sandra with us whenever we're together. Let's do a mother-daughter weekend."

Alert: Don't be afraid to ruffle a parent's feathers. She'll be flattered that you want to be with her one-on-one.

··· SCENARIO ···

"What do you mean you're not asking your cousin to be in the bridal party? You grew up together."

What's Going on Here: You did, indeed, grow up together. You were forced to play with her when you didn't want to and had to do whatever she wanted. Excluding family holiday celebrations, you saw less and less of each other as you grew up. By the teen years you tolerated your cousin, but you had nothing in common. You'd feel like a hypocrite if she was in your wedding party, and it would mean having to leave out a dear friend.

Response: "I know how you feel, Mother, but I can't ask her. She's not part of my life anymore. We decided we want only our friends, and we're not changing our minds." In fact, you can add, "No one else in the family is in the bridal party other than the maid of honor and best man."

Alert: Be prepared for hard feelings and perturbed relatives, but that will be easier to face than a cousin you barely relate to walking down the aisle on your wedding day.

··· SCENARIO ···

*"Surprise! Your honeymoon is on us," your
parents or future in-laws e-mail, sending a
link to an extravagant tropical getaway.*

What's Going on Here: You noticed some hesitation on their part when you and your betrothed hinted at a sensible, low-cost honeymoon. The e-mail, with the enticing photos, is their attempt to convince you to change plans.

Response: "Thank you, but we have a different honeymoon in mind."

Alert: Don't be swayed by magnanimous offers that could dictate your marital beginnings and open doors to parents directing your new life. Once opened, they are difficult to close.

··· SCENARIO ···

*"You need to call your sister-in-law and make
amends before she becomes more incensed,"
your father says in an accusatory tone.*

What's Going on Here: Your father will try anything to keep things amicable between you and your siblings. He knows your sister-in-law mandates how your brother relates to the rest of the family. He assumes you said or did something to offend her.

Response: "I am not apologizing for something I didn't do. If anything, she should be calling me. Maybe I'll call my brother at some point and talk it over with him."

Alert: When you are the one always making the first move to smooth family differences, it's probably time to step back. It's not your sole responsibility to keep the family peace; keeping family ties strong takes more than one willing family member.

··· SCENARIO ···

The inevitable tug of war begins when your mother announces, as she always does, "Thanksgiving dinner is at five o'clock." She neither acknowledges nor accepts excuses, nor will she move dinner or dinnertime to accommodate spouses and their families.

What's Going on Here: She's refused your request to host Thanksgiving since you got married. You want to prove to your parents, your friends, and yourself that you can do it. Or maybe you want to sit at the head of the table, your table, on this important family holiday. You want to feel like a grown-up on Thanksgiving, but your mother doesn't seem to care how you feel. She's obstinate, but that shouldn't be news to you.

Response: "No, Mother, this year Thanksgiving dinner is at my house at five o'clock."

Alert: It is possible to change tradition. Nothing is etched in stone except epitaphs in cemeteries. Although parents may balk initially, they generally acclimate to their adult offspring's wishes as long as they are included.

··· SCENARIO ···

"You need to buy stock with the money you inherited from your grandfather. Let me help you decide."

What's Going on Here: Your grandfather left you a sizable sum of money. You know exactly how you want to spend it, and it's not investing in the stock market. Your heart is set on a down payment for a house, a new car, a much-needed vacation, or a stylish new wardrobe.

Response: "No, thank you."

Alert: This is your windfall to invest (or squander) as you wish, not as a parent thinks you should. If there's some left over, you can consult with your parent on how to invest it, assuming that's what you decide.

··· SCENARIO ···

"Take a look at this offer!" your father e-mails, with a link to a new car for sale. Minutes later, another e-mail comes in: "Here's another." Other e-mails follow.

What's Going on Here: You've artfully dodged your father's snide comments about your beat-up used car, but he's betting he can get your attention and convince you to make a "smart purchase" via e-mail. It's one thing to have physical space from him and ignore his phone calls, but the e-mails flooding your inbox put you on edge.

Response: "No, Dad, I told you I'm not in a place to consider this." Add that if he would like to chat about something else, you're all ears.

Alert: Some parents can't halt the need to manage aspects of their children's lives. Let a parent know that the topic is closed without cutting off communication.

··· SCENARIO ···

"Can't you let him sit in the backseat? He's old enough, and we're only going a short distance," your parent tells you as you struggle to get your squirming three-year-old into his car seat.

What's Going on Here: Your parent may be unaware that safety precautions and equipment have changed dramatically since he or she drove babies and toddlers. A gentle update may be all that's required.

Response: "No, he has to be buckled into his seat. It's the law."

Alert: No matter how persuasive a parent, when it comes to your child's safety, you are in charge.

··· SCENARIO ···

"How about I take the children swimming so you can have the afternoon to yourself?"

What's Going on Here: Your heart skips a beat at your mother's offer. You need a break, but she's the last person on earth you would entrust with your children near water. She's easily distracted; you imagine her in her bathing suit chatting it up with someone she's introduced herself to. She swivels her body away from the water to answer her new acquaintance's question while your darling children dog-paddle alone in the water. But who are you to tell a parent he or she can't spend time with the grandchildren?

Response: "That is so nice of you. Let's all go." Or, "Thanks, but not today."

Alert: It's no day off if you are going to worry yourself sick the entire time the children are in your mother's care. Saying no moves boundaries into your comfort zone.

··· SCENARIO ···

"I told Owen he could watch one episode before bed," your father, who's visiting for the holidays, informs you. "One hour won't kill him!"

What's Going on Here: You love that your dad is a doting grand-father, but what started out as him handing out extra pieces of candy and buying ice cream sundaes has turned into full-blown disregard for your house rules.

Response: "I know you have Owen's best interests at heart, but you cannot undermine my role as a parent. Please do not give him permission without checking with me."

Alert: It's natural for parents to clash with their own parents or in-laws regarding parenting styles. Often, how you were raised can be quite different from how you parent. Grand-parents are important family connectors who need occasional reminders that they need to respect your rules.

··· SCENARIO ···

"Where's the hat we got Logan for his birthday?"
your father writes on a photo you posted of your
toddler son. "He looks cold over there!" Later, he
texts: "Send us a pic of the little guy in his gift?"

What's Going on Here: Keeping faraway relatives abreast of your children's lives is a snap with social media, but it's also become a space for nitpicking comments and unwanted scrutiny. It's hard to get a sense of your father's tone in the comment, but you immediately feel as if you messed up by not posting a picture of your son in the hat.

Response: "I promise you, Logan loves his hat! You'll see for yourself over the holidays."

Alert: Distance can be problematic in emotionally close families, and your father could be feeling left out. No need to drop everything you're doing right there to find the hat for an impromptu photo session—a firm reassurance should quell your parent's fear that he's missing out.

··· SCENARIO ···

"You're not really letting her cut her hair like that,
are you?" your mother asks after your teenaged
daughter announces her plans for a buzz cut.
"You can't possibly allow her to do that."

What's Going on Here: When you were growing up, your mother would have never let you do anything drastic with your appearance—piercings, bold hairstyles, and tattoos were forbidden. Your parenting style has been much different, and the buzz cut is one more reason for your mother to denounce your parenting style.

Response: "We made an informed decision as parents to let her. I realize you think our decision is wrong."

Alert: Acknowledging a parent's disapproval is often enough to make the subject go away.

··· **SCENARIO** ···

"What do you mean you're not flying home for Easter? That's ridiculous. I'm sending you airfare," your mother e-mails.

What's Going on Here: You've explained you're short on funds and are working on turning things around. Since your mother has discovered how to transfer money on her smartphone, she thinks she can "will" you home by fronting your airfare. If you accept, you will feel guilty about the cost and feel obligated to run errands and do the bulk of the cooking once you get home.

Response: "I really would like to spend Easter with everyone. I know you're upset and that you want to help, but I need to turn my finances around myself. Please don't cover my flight again."

Alert: Parents have difficulty accepting change. Emphasize it's not personal and it's more important to you to be financially independent than to adhere to the family's Easter tradition.

··· SCENARIO ···

*"You can't possibly be adopting. Don't you
want to give us biological grandchildren?"*

What's Going on Here: Your parents or in-laws can't fathom having
grandchildren that don't share their eyes or their uncle's ath-
leticism. Having children naturally is not an option unless you
undergo more costly fertility treatments, which your parents
have offered to pay for. They don't comprehend the emotional
"costs" of IVF. You've firmly decided that you want to adopt.

Response: "Our children will love you no matter what. Please
support us."

Alert: Adoption is not a second-best option. Children raised
in warm homes by adoptive parents form loving, nurturing
connections to their relatives.

··· SCENARIO ···

*"We're concerned about how you're managing
your investments," your parents call to say.
"Give us your login information, and we can
take a look and help you sort it out."*

What's Going on Here: Yes, it is handy that you can view your
financial activity online, but no, that does not mean it's
something for your overly worried parents to comb through.
They're letting the helicopter tendencies that were in full force
when you were a teen get the best of them.

Response: "No, I'm perfectly capable of managing my money. I
will come to you if I have any concerns or questions."

Alert: Studies show that younger adult Americans handle money much differently than their parents, from savings accounts to credit cards. If you don't want your parents taking over, you have a right to refuse their advice—no explanation needed.

··· SCENARIO ···

"Don't you think Michele should spend more time job hunting?" your father-in-law asks.

What's Going on Here: Michele is your sister-in-law, and you don't want to get in the middle of any father-daughter, mother-daughter conflicts. Agree, and you're asking for trouble.

Response: "I don't have an opinion." Or, "I don't know." Or, "I haven't thought about it."

Alert: You take the chance that your in-law will repeat what you say to your sister-in-law, who will be displeased with you for taking sides. In families, who's aligned with whom can change in a flash. Be careful.

··· SCENARIO ···

"What do you want me to bring Friday for dinner?" your mother or mother-in-law asks.

What's Going on Here: Since you had babies, the five of you have had a standing dinner date on Friday nights. The children are older now, in school, and participate in scheduled activities.

Response: "Nothing. We have to stop Friday night dinners. We want and need more time alone with just us and the kids. We will see you lots of other times, don't worry." (She will.)

Alert: Time alone as a family is your choice. Your mother or mother-in-law will feel abandoned initially, but she has little choice but to adjust. The first time you announce the change, soften the blow by extending an invitation to one of the children's upcoming activities the following week.

··· SCENARIO ···

"I'm begging you to invite your sister and Gary."

What's Going on Here: A parent is trying to orchestrate your relationship with a sibling. Your sister and her partner are unreliable and inconsiderate; they arrive late enough to ruin a meal you've cooked or to make you late for an appointment, and they never apologize. If a parent pleads, she knows that you've been tolerating your sister and brother-in-law's selfish behavior for a long time. Your parent is struggling to keep the family unit whole.

Response: "I'm not putting myself in that position again."

Alert: Enough already of being the "good" sibling. You don't have to take indirect insults to calm or appease a parent. Excluding the offenders may open their eyes to the reality that they can't act as if you have no feelings. It may be rough going for a while, but the discomfort will sort itself out in time.

· · · · · · · · · · · ·

Sibling Strife

Sibling relationships contain a host of different dynamics. Some siblings grow up close, bonded by true friendship. Others have contentious or competitive relationships. Some siblings coddle or protect each other, and this "watching out" extends into adulthood. Others feel guilty as adults for not getting along as children.

Whatever the nature of your relationship, childhoods affect how you respond to each other as adults, often stemming from patterns built over time.

Whether a sibling's reasons behind a particular ask are good—such as wishing what's best for you—or are motivated by selfishness or bossiness, for instance, how you respond to a request can significantly impact your life and the feelings you and your sibling have for each other.

··· SCENARIO ···

"We're having girls' night out with Mom next Friday. You'll join us, won't you?"

What's Going on Here: You've had a dinner-and-a-movie ritual with family members for most of your adult life, and those evenings are excruciating. Your sisters are only too happy to tell you what you do wrong with your social life, with your makeup, and at your job. You have told them that this bothers you, but their behavior hasn't changed. You don't want to be the one who ruins the tradition, and every year you think this night will be different. Face it: it won't be.

Response: "I can't be there." You don't have to explain or make excuses, because you are a grown-up.

Alert: Wishful thinking does not prevent siblings (or parents) from insulting you. Chances are, they have been behaving this way for so long that they are not apt to stop.

··· SCENARIO ···

A group e-mail message from your sister: "Dad's Birthday Party Plan." Although you had both spoken briefly about planning something together, your sister has decided she's in charge. Among the tasks she's assigned to you: design the invitations, find a caterer, bake dad's favorite cake.

What's Going on Here: Your sister has always been the bossy one. You'll admit she is good at being in charge, and in many cases in the past, you've deferred to her wishes. But after her e-mail, you're now dreading a party you were once looking forward to.

Response: "I'm not okay with this plan. Let's discuss something different in person." Or, "What's a good time to call you?"

Alert: A sibling may not even realize her assertiveness is prickly. Taking the conversation out of e-mail is the best way for her to hear you and your wishes about how you want to contribute to the event.

··· SCENARIO ···

"The baby is due at the end of July. Will you stay with the children while I'm in the hospital?" your sister asks again.

What's Going on Here: Caring for the older children is what you do in your family when a newborn arrives. You feel obligated, but your responsibilities have changed since the last baby was born: you have a job, or your children are older and must be driven to activities, or you are taking care of a sick relative. Or, you don't want to.

Response: "I know I stayed with Lizzie when Ian was born, but it's impossible for me to do that now."

Alert: Even for major life events, give yourself permission to say no, especially if you've pitched in on other occasions. It doesn't always have to be you.

··· **SCENARIO** ···

"Your baby is the most beautiful child," your sister says as soon as she steps into the nursery. "Time for that selfie with Auntie Stephanie!"

What's Going on Here: Your sister has been trying to orchestrate your firstborn's Internet debut ever since she first saw him at the hospital. She wants to post something and hopes you'll finally give in. You have your reasons for not wanting your child's picture online.

Response: "Still no. There will be plenty of time for photos in the future."

Alert: Your sister may think you're being ridiculous for not wanting to share your baby on social media. Be happy that she's elated about becoming an aunt, but don't change your mind because she questions your choice.

••• SCENARIO •••

"It's been months since Grandma died.
Will you divide her belongings as you see
fit and send us whatever? We want a token
that will remind us of Grandma."

What's Going on Here: You live the closest, so you've been elected to sort through your grandmother's belongings and divide them among your siblings. You can pretty much count on one of your siblings being unhappy with how you divvy up Grandma's dishes and jewelry. They say they don't care, but they do. In the end, agreeing will be more painful than insisting you won't do it by yourself.

Response: Save heartache and bad feelings by saying something like "I will not go through Grandma's things by myself. One of you will have to fly here and we'll do it together."

Alert: Don't be bamboozled into a task that frequently leads to unnecessary tension and conflict in families. No matter how equitably you think you handle the distribution, someone will feel cheated when you unilaterally make all the decisions.

••• SCENARIO •••

"Can you help Mom and Dad pack up the
basement on Saturday? My kids have soccer
(baseball, football, tennis) tournaments
(games, practice)," your sister asks.

What's Going on Here: Your "excuse" sibling is doing what she does best. If she isn't using her children to exempt her, she'll have a bridal shower or wedding to attend, a guest in from out of town, or a project she can't possibly put on hold.

Response: "No, I can't be there Saturday. How about we both go over on Sunday?"

Alert: Answering a question with a question catches people unprepared with an excuse. Since you know you will help your parents at some point, changing the schedule may lock in your sister.

··· SCENARIO ···

"Help me finish building the deck this weekend?" your brother asks.

What's Going on Here: You helped when he started the deck. After the first day of manual labor, you were miserable and achy. Your brother, a talented craftsman, has been hounding you for not returning.

Response: "Clearly, carpentry is not in my skill set. Dad is a much better assistant. I'll provide the celebratory twelve-pack of beer when you're finished."

Alert: You shouldn't feel "in trouble" for turning down a request that is beyond your ability or physical stamina.

··· SCENARIO ···

"Can you revise my résumé?"

What's Going on Here: You're close with your younger sister, but sense she's come to use you as her staff. In the past, you didn't mind—you helped her with her homework, bought supplies for her new apartment, sorted out her dating life—but she's started to turn to you for things she can do herself.

Response: "I'll read it over after you edit and draft it."

Alert: The essential give-and-take between siblings, if excessive, can develop into dependency. Jump in to help avoid a major mistake, but step back to encourage self-sufficiency.

··· SCENARIO ···

"I hate to ask you again, but could you send a check for the repairs on Mom's roof?"

What's Going on Here: One of your siblings calls to ask you to foot the whole bill for a parent's new roof, new car, airline tickets, or a holiday gift. This sibling has it in mind that you are the rich relative, a bottomless pit of money—the family's private banker.

Response: "We all need to chip in." Or, "I can't do it alone—I can only pay half" (if true); "I'm strapped myself" (if true). Or, "My money's invested" (if true).

Alert: Short-circuit anticipated contributions by insisting the expense be divided or by compromising to reach a fair solution. A *no* is often the only way that will happen. When it starts to feel as if relatives love your money more than they love you, it's time to stop supporting the family.

··· SCENARIO ···

*Your brother calls: "I can't pay my rent this
month and also pay my credit card bill. Can
you help me out? Last time, I promise."*

What's Going on Here: You and your brother are trying to mend
your rocky relationship, and his request makes it harder. Are
you inclined to say yes in an effort to make amends or assuage
your guilt for not being more supportive? How much will the
loan impact you? Will you have to struggle to pay your own
bills? Will you have to sacrifice a weekend trip or dinner out
that you've been planning? Will you end up back where you
started, as kids fighting with each other?

Response: "I'm sorry, but I can't right now."

Alert: Saying yes and feeling taken advantage of could damage
a shaky sibling relationship further. When you agree to loan
money, consider that you might be enabling a sibling's indis-
criminate spending.

··· SCENARIO ···

*"Can you lend me $3,000?" your sister
texts. "I'm DESPERATE."*

What's Going on Here: The last time your sister asked you for a
favor it was to copy your notes in high school. Sent with little
information, her text comes as a shock and sends you into
serious worry mode.

Response: "We need to talk about what's going on."

Alert: A sibling's crisis can feel like your own. Take a deep breath and get the facts so you can be as helpful as possible beyond a bailout.

··· SCENARIO ···

Your sister wants to know if you will call Dad to convince him to change his mind and join the family for dinner.

What's Going on Here: Your father and your brother-in-law had a nasty verbal disagreement—a shouting match, in fact. You will only wind up embroiled in a dispute that had nothing to do with you in the first place.

Response: "I'm not going to be the intermediary."

Alert: Stay as far away as you can from family feuds that don't directly involve you—there'll be enough that do. Trying to be the peacemaker rarely earns a reward.

··· SCENARIO ···

Your brother comments on a photo you posted, a harmless selfie of you at the gym: "Woah what happened to Dumbo?!" he says, resurrecting his childhood nickname for you.

What's Going on Here: He was naturally thin while you struggled with your weight. Memories of your brother's mean comments come rushing back. Even if you are on good terms as adult siblings, call him on it.

Response: Message him privately: "You don't seem to see how difficult your teasing was for me when we were younger. I certainly don't appreciate it now."

Alert: Sweeping insensitive comments under the rug or allowing them to go unchallenged won't make them stop.

··· SCENARIO ···

*Your brother organizes a family trip every
year and gets irritated when you don't follow
his instructions immediately. He calls every
day to remind you: "You need to buy your
airline tickets before prices skyrocket."*

What's Going on Here: It irks your brother that you wait until you have the money in hand, even if the price increases, before purchasing. You don't want the expense on your credit card this month.

Response: "Don't worry. We will get there. The kids are very excited to see you."

Alert: You know your brother means well, but you also know he's a control freak. The pestering is *his* problem, not yours.

··· SCENARIO ···

*Today's question from your sister: "Any suggestions
on how I can bring Jim back into my life?"*

What's Going on Here: Every day she has a question or something she needs your help with: the kids won't do their homework, she can't figure out how to get both children to sports practice on different fields at the same time, she needs a job, the recipe doesn't taste as good as when you make it . . . She thinks she's the only one with problems, the only one with too much to do. She leans on you to pick up her pieces, to listen to her every tale of woe. She's always had some calamity in her life, and you've always come to her rescue, but dealing with her problems has gotten old.

Response: "No, I've got my own crises today."

Alert: Reduce the time you spend with or talk to high-maintenance siblings so that you have emotional reserves for your own tasks and problems. With some family, no matter how much you do, it's not enough.

. . . .

Those Other Relatives!

Within the family, your reputation for diligence precedes you. You've been branded as the faithful family fixer. You buy the gifts, send the flowers, visit the hospital, solve technology problems, grocery shop with your great-aunt, and handle emergencies. Relatives assume you will be in charge or take care of what needs to be done. Quite possibly, you've convinced yourself that things don't get done unless you do them. Don't you often think you're the only dependable grown-up in the family? Trouble is, your whole family thinks that way, too.

There's a sense of obligation to be more polite with people you're not as closely linked to as you are with your parents, in-laws, and siblings. When "those other relatives" are particularly bothersome, you may feel less comfortable turning down a request—especially when, on the surface, it seems like an isolated one.

Parents and siblings are most likely to be sources of unconditional love, even after you turn down a request or change a tradition. With cousins, cousins twice removed, sisters- and brothers-in-law, and aunts and uncles, it can be tricky to retain positive, healthy relations. When your guilt-trip signal flashes red in your mind, be cautious. By regularly complying with every relative's request, you could end up feeling taken advantage of. It is possible to stay in your family's good graces and still turn down "those other relatives."

··· SCENARIO ···

"My daughter needs a last-minute pianist for her oboe recital. "You'll help us out, right?" your aunt asks.

What's Going on Here: You remember how stressful it was being a young musician on the eve of a performance. Your aunt knows that you're a fairly accomplished pianist, and she's confident you will play for your young cousin. You will need to find time to learn the music and practice together.

Response: "No, I'm not the best person. I'm sure you can find a professional musician."

Alert: Agree and you wind up roped into something time-consuming that you really don't want to do.

··· SCENARIO ···

Uncle Ned asks, "Let's go to Disney World, my treat. Should I get tickets for the children's spring break or during their summer vacation?"

What's Going on Here: Your uncle is trying to buy your loyalty and love. It's an almost irresistible gift, but one you will pay for many times over. For starters, you will have to be nice to him, his airhead wife, and his impossible children the whole time you're together. He will dictate what rides to take and what sights to see while boastfully reminding you what a great guy he is.

Response: "Thanks, Uncle Ned, but we're saving Disney World for when the children are older."

Alert: You will be in Uncle Ned's debt and forced to suffer his superiority for longer than you can imagine. Before you accept, decide if the trip is worth all the groveling you'll have to do.

··· SCENARIO ···

"You shouldn't bring Hugh. I know you're engaged, but Grandma will be horrified," your favorite aunt or cousin somberly says before a big holiday party. "You know how she is—she can't get her head around all that LGBT stuff."

What's Going on Here: It's safe to say you are easily among your grandmother's favorite grandchildren, but upon coming out, she has refused to talk to you about it.

Response: "If I can't bring Hugh, I will not attend this year. This is the person I love, and Grandma will have to accept that I'm gay."

Alert: In some families, everyone bows to one relative who believes what she wants is an "earned" right. Yes-prone family members fall into the habit of kowtowing to that relative's wishes. You don't have to.

··· SCENARIO ···

Aunt Judy is about to tell you—pound by pound— how she lost weight. "Darling, I have to tell you about a marvelous new weight-loss regimen."

What's Going on Here: After trying dozens of different diets yourself, you're not going to get into it with Aunt Judy at a family party. With her svelte new figure, she's going to make you feel terrible (you're embarrassed by your still-chunky self anyway) and, what's worse, convince you to test her new diet program right there and then.

Response: "Aunt Judy, you look great, but we're not going to talk about diets today."

Alert: Avoid topics that you know will make you feel bad by declaring them off-limits.

··· SCENARIO ···

"What happened to the guy you brought to the party last year? I liked him," your uncle says in front of your new boyfriend.

What's Going on Here: Ribbing each other is "what your family does," but your uncle has no filter and thinks his question is harmless and amusing. You're embarrassed and annoyed.

Response: "I don't think that's funny, Uncle Sid." Scowl, pat him on the shoulder, and circulate with other guests.

Alert: Direct language is the best way to shut down insensitive relatives. You'll be more upset if you don't say something to let him know that he's way off base.

··· SCENARIO ···

Your second cousin e-mails or private messages you on Facebook: "You're an English professor— can Simone e-mail you her college essay? She has to submit it tomorrow or she won't be eligible for a scholarship. I'm sending it right now."

What's Going on Here: You know how frustrated your cousin and his daughter must feel. You also know they could use the scholarship money. You have sixty papers to grade by the semester's end on Monday. They could have reached out to you sooner. Will they see you as selfish if you say no?

Response: "I am swamped. Isn't there a teacher or college counselor at her school who can check it first thing in the morning?"

Alert: Their panic is not your panic. If you wish, offer to read the next essay, but stipulate how much advance notice you need.

⋯ SCENARIO ⋯

*"At the reunion, you and the girls will be
in charge of dinner as always, right?"
your uncle calls to remind you.*

What's Going on Here: Year after year, it's exactly the same: the women cook while the men and boys play touch football outside. You've always wanted to join the guys.

Response: "Actually, I'm going to suit up and kick your butt on the field, Uncle Charlie."

Alert: Keep your comment light, but let it be known that you won't be forced into jobs simply based on gender bias. You may inspire other females in the family to do the same or encourage male relatives to opt for kitchen assignments.

⋯ SCENARIO ⋯

*Your great-aunt calls minutes after learning that
your minister is unable to officiate at your upcoming
wedding. "You know, your cousin's brother-in-law
is ordained and can step in," she says. "I have his
number here, I'll give him a call and it's done."*

What's Going on Here: You are scrambling to get your wedding plans in order but hate the idea of someone you've never met marrying you.

Response: "Thank you, I appreciate your call, but no. I'll get back to you if we can't find someone."

Alert: People with the best intentions don't think about your preferences or how you plan to solve your problem . . . and often don't ask. They want to be the "hero."

··· SCENARIO ···

Your cousin's mother passed away and she wants to buy one of your burial plots. "We don't have a grave for Mom. Possible?" she asks.

What's Going on Here: You, too, are grieving your aunt's death, but the unexpected request will surely distress you down the road. The remaining family graves were designated so your mother and you could be near your dad.

Response: "No, our family agreed years ago that one space would be my mother's and one mine. I am happy to help you arrange for one somewhere else in the cemetery."

Alert: A sensitive time may feel like the right time to grant an urgent request, but it isn't always the most prudent decision.

··· SCENARIO ···

"Thanks for taking care of the funeral. I need $2,500 for a security deposit on a new apartment," your late sister's boyfriend texts. "And money to pay the movers," he texts an instant later.

What's Going on Here: It's only been a few weeks since your sister suddenly passed away and the family is still in shock. Her longtime, live-in boyfriend is strapped for cash and turns to you, even though you two are not close. You understand he's upset about having to move out of the apartment they shared. You don't know yet how much money your sister had or where it might be.

Response: "I don't have the money to help you."

Alert: When someone dies, it can sometimes feel as if people come out of the woodwork wanting a piece of the inheritance pie, if there is one. People rightly or wrongly feel as if they are entitled to something and believe you are the person to approve their requests. This is an unfortunate situation, but it is not your responsibility to be the financial safety net for everyone who asks.

··· **SCENARIO** ···

"You're voting for [insert politician here], on Tuesday, right?" your second cousin writes on your Facebook wall, assuming you belong to the same political party.

What's Going on Here: Upon "friending" a relative, you've come to discover his or her social media canvassing is far more charged than yours. It doesn't bug you to see her opinions pop up daily on your news feed, but you certainly don't share her perspective and don't want to get involved or end up in a public debate.

Response: None.

Alert: On social media, you can silently walk away. If you say something that antagonizes your cousin, you open yourself to others criticizing your views online. Unless a relative shows up at your doorstep waving campaign pamphlets and spewing opinions, it's best to let it lie.

··· SCENARIO ···

*Your niece comes to you. "Can you talk to
my mom for me?" she asks. "She's so strict.
She won't let me go out on a date with Josh.
Can you tell her she should? If she hears it
from you maybe she'll change her mind."*

What's Going on Here: You've come to love how your family members see you as the one to go to for guidance, and you see yourself as a good leader. But will saying yes create friction with your sister-in-law? Is your niece taking advantage of your usual willingness to take her side?

Response: "I'd like to help you, honey, but it's not my place. I'm here if you want to talk out the problem."

Alert: It may feel special to be the family member people approach for guidance, but it's not always appropriate for you to respond.

··· SCENARIO ···

*You knew it would happen. The instant your
wife Snapchats you and the kids enjoying
the new trampoline, you get a text from your
cousins who live nearby. "Looks like you've
got your own little amusement park over
there! Can we come over with the kids?"*

What's Going on Here: Just as company flooded your house when you got the playground set, barbecue, or high-definition television, relatives once again see your home as theirs. At first you enjoyed family stopping by, but it's starting to feel as if you are the family's entertainment center and caterer.

Response: "We need a day to ourselves. Let's set up an afternoon to be together soon. You guys can bring that casserole the kids love!"

Alert: To avoid creating family tension, find a gentle way around a flat-out *no*. Suggesting relatives contribute something sends the message that there needs to be some fairness.

··· SCENARIO ···

"Let's give Brianna a baby shower together."

What's Going on Here: You wanted to give Cousin Brianna a shower by yourself. She's more like a sister than a cousin. You believe a joint shower diminishes your role as her best and closest friend and doesn't tell Brianna how important she is to you. Refusing another family member might set off a whole chain reaction within the family—but it might not. And, in the excitement of a new baby, your decision will likely become insignificant.

Response: "No, I really want to do this myself. I've been thinking about it since Brianna got married. It's something I have to do. I hope you understand."

Alert: Once you've made it clear how meaningful hosting the event is to you, do what pleases you. The others can and will give their own shower(s) if they feel as compelled and committed as you are.

··· SCENARIO ···

"What do you mean, you're not going to Jill's gallery opening? She's worked for years to get a show of her photos, and you're not going to be there to support her? You have to go. What kind of person are you?"

What's Going on Here: Someone in your family badgers you, refusing to accept your *no*. Your reasons could range from having something else scheduled to not caring about Jill or her photography, but you don't say this and don't want to get into a screaming match. Stay as calm as you can to prevent the situation from escalating to the point of your saying something you will be sorry for later.

Response: "It's not possible, and that's the way it is. I'll stop in to see Jill's show another time" (if you will).

Alert: When the pressure is on for you to relent, repeat to yourself, "I will not give in, I will not give in," to help you stick to your refusal.

··· SCENARIO ···

You unwrap your aunt and uncle's Christmas gift and freeze. It's a baptism dress, obviously intended for your baby daughter. "It should fit if you have her christened soon," Aunt Courtney beams.

What's Going on Here: You and your partner don't intend to raise your child in the same religion you both grew up in. You would be the first in your family to do so, making your decision all the more shocking to your relatives.

Response: "You are too kind, but no, we won't be needing this. Our plans don't include a baptism."

Alert: This won't be the first time you'll hear objections to your choice, but committing to a firm *no* is the only path to ultimate acceptance or tolerance when a religious choice differs from your family's beliefs.

··· SCENARIO ···

"I don't know how to access the cloud," your great-uncle says at a family gathering. "I'm not hip like you young guys. Can you show me?"

What's Going on Here: Your great-uncle thinks flattery is his ticket for getting you to help with a task you have no time, interest, or energy for. You barely know how yourself.

Response: "Go online to find a step-by-step guide. They are easy to follow and more instructive than I would be."

Alert: Being part of a generation that has a greater understanding of tech concepts doesn't mean you have a duty to teach them.

··· SCENARIO ···

"Will you pick up a gift for Kristin's graduation and wrap it for me? I'm at a loss as to what to get her."

What's Going on Here: The family views you as the Martha Stewart of shopping and gift wrapping, which may or may not be accurate. You're having a hard enough time figuring out what you will buy the graduate. Finding something for someone else in your family to give is too big a drain on your creativity. More to the point, if a relative can hoodwink you into doing her shopping and wrapping, how much the better for her.

Response: "I don't know what we are giving her. You're on your own with this one."

Alert: Abandon the need to rescue everyone in the family who asks. And, as quickly as you can, try to dispel the myth that you do anything exceptionally well.

··· SCENARIO ···

"We want to relocate Uncle Eddie into an assisted living complex, but we don't know where to begin," says a cousin. You haven't had contact in over a year, but she wants your input.

What's Going on Here: The questions are implied: What do you know about such facilities? Will you research on the Internet, call the insurance company, pick up some caregiving books, go visit some places? The family knows that it's in your nature to volunteer helpful ideas and information.

Response: "It's foreign territory to me too" (if it is). Or, "We had such bad experiences with my mom/dad/aunt/uncle, I'm afraid I'm no help" (if true). Recommend a person with experience or knowledge if you know someone who can help.

Alert: Exercise self-restraint or you could find yourself alone in making the arrangements to resettle Uncle Eddie.

··· SCENARIO ···

*"You'll take the pictures at your
cousin's wedding, won't you?"*

What's Going on Here: Could be an aunt, a sister-in-law, or the bride's mother asking, the assumption being that you want this scary assignment. You're good, but you are not a professional photographer—you don't have a backup camera or a staff holding lights. You shoot pictures for fun and for an occasional gift. Think this one through: What if the batteries wear down just as the groom feeds your cousin the first piece of wedding cake? Nervous yet? When will you get to dance or chat? If you want to do something creative for your cousin, decorate the getaway car or write your own toast.

Response: "No. That's a responsibility I will not assume."

Alert: When the need for pitch-perfect performance is high and the responsibility weighty, advise the family to hire a "real" photographer or appropriate professional to do the required job.

··· SCENARIO ···

*"I need you to do me a huge favor," your aunt
begins. "Can my daughter live with you for
a little while, only until she finds a job?"*

What's Going on Here: The last time you interacted with your cousin was at your sweet-sixteen party. You feel pressured to go along with your aunt's request. Your cousin and aunt would be thrilled, but knowing the stay could last months, you would fume silently.

Response: "I'm happy to help her with her job hunt, but she can't stay with me."

Alert: When you agree to make someone else happy at the expense of your own personal freedom, feelings of resentment are likely to build.

··· SCENARIO ···

"You're going to wait a year to start Will in kindergarten, aren't you?" your sister-in-law says.

What's Going on Here: In the guise of a question, a sister-in-law, aunt, uncle, or cousin is telling you what you should do without being asked. This relative is insinuating that your son is not mature enough to handle school, making a hard call all the more difficult.

Response: "We haven't decided what we're doing."

Alert: Family members seem to feel they have every right to offer opinions about your children. Ignore them or you will be in continuous turmoil about your parenting choices.

· · · · · · · · · · ·

No, Darling

In the range of difficulty, refusing the person you love ranks as high on the scale as refusing a parent. There's that same sense of wanting to be there and not wanting to disappoint. You float between the desire to make him or her happy and feeling perturbed at not being happy yourself—often because you are in perpetual motion or feel unenthusiastic about what's asked of you. As many partners communicate via tech like text or e-mail, there's plenty of room for knee-jerk responses or misinterpretations that can lead to conflict.

Saying no to a spouse or partner is a bit of a struggle because when you're in love you tend to give in easily. Or, you may say yes because you want to avoid an argument, compensate for devoting more time to work or the children than to your partner, or believe saying yes keeps the relationship strong. On the flip side, when you fall into a pattern of agreeing, the relationship becomes imbalanced and you open yourself up to frustration. That's risky. Isn't it time to speak up and make life as a twosome more equitable?

··· SCENARIO ···

Your partner texts:
"Coming home now. Start dinner."

What's Going on Here: You work from home, and your spouse does not. She's come to see that as a reason for you to get food on the table—even though your workload is as hefty as hers. The curt, demanding text makes you feel like your only option is to comply.

Response: Text back: "No, I'm swamped. Can you pick something up? Or we'll order in."

Alert: If the pattern has been that you almost always prepare dinner (do the laundry, get the car washed), break it. There's more than one way to fix a meal or get chores done.

··· SCENARIO ···

"I love you.
We haven't known each other long, but I
want you to marry me. Will you?"

What's Going on Here: After a few whirlwind months of dating, you're crazy about him. You think it might work in the long term, but your sixth sense is telling you that it is too soon for you to make such a life-altering commitment. Plus, he has a few personal quirks you are not sure you can live with.

Response: "I love you, too. Give me some time."

Alert: Any reservation is serious and therefore worth a stall. If something about the man or woman urging you to spend your life together nags at you, wait to answer the big question. Life-changing decisions can be delayed.

··· SCENARIO ···

"Can you come home earlier tonight?
Blow off your dinner meeting. We don't
spend time together anymore."

What's Going on Here: You agree with your significant other. As much as you want to, you'd kick yourself if you succumbed to the plea. The late meeting is crucial.

Response: "I miss you too. I know it's unclear why this project is so demanding of my time. We'll plan a special weekend after the assignment is put to bed."

Alert: Avoid spiraling into a defensive argument about the rigors of your job and accusing him or her of not understanding.

··· SCENARIO ···

You sit down to breakfast and your husband
is already glued to Fantasy Football on his
phone. "Oh, no! I have to text Ron. He won't
believe what just happened," he says.

What's Going on Here: At every meal, your partner's cell phone sits next to his knife and spoon. His eyes are on it constantly; he never looks at or speaks to you directly. You didn't mind at first, but his obsession has made you feel completely disconnected as a couple. You know it's important to him, but it irks you.

Response: "Let's at least eat breakfast first. I don't want to sit here, ignored, and have a conversation with my toast."

Alert: When you put your cell phones aside and talk, you never know what might happen—some surprising information or intimacy may be shared. It's possible your spouse is so engrossed that he doesn't realize you feel ignored and alone. Researchers found that when looking at "problematic use" of cell phones—that is, when users turn to screens at rude or inappropriate times—they themselves feel less socially bonded to others than they would if they stopped using the phone as a replacement for face-to-face communication.

··· SCENARIO ···

"Honey, when you're shopping today, buy golf balls."

What's Going on Here: You are a devoted wife who doesn't complain when her husband plays golf—which is much more often than you would like, leaving you with the bulk of the child and household responsibilities. Having to do his shopping is pouring salt on the wound.

Response: "Not happening."

Alert: No matter how much you love your spouse, there is no need for you to shop for gear or equipment that encourages his absences.

··· SCENARIO ···

"Wow, people are really blowing up about this breaking news out of Washington," your wife says. She's scrolling away on her phone as soon as you've stepped out for a date you've been planning all week. "Do you want to see?"

What's Going on Here: You both agreed to dedicate the evening to each other. But immediately, she's rivetted to her phone, her usual distraction.

Response: "The news can wait. Let's switch off our phones and focus on us. I made reservations at your favorite restaurant."

Alert: Responding with an irritated "No!" could push her away from a much-needed personal conversation. Find a gentle way to emphasize that being glued to the phone is unacceptable tonight.

··· SCENARIO ···

"Why are you still friends with Derek on social media?" your husband asks. "It's weird to me. Delete him, please."

What's Going on Here: Your husband doesn't maintain friendships with any of his exes and doesn't grasp why you can stay on good terms with yours. You see the relationship as ancient history but want to stay in touch for whatever reasons. You wonder: Is your husband overreacting? Jealous?

Response: "We barely interact online. I am married and committed to you 100 percent. You know that. There's no need to sever my social media connection to Derek."

Alert: If time has passed and there truly are no emotional strings attached, assure your spouse he has no reason to be jealous.

⋯ SCENARIO ⋯

Your ex-husband asks you to call his mother to discuss a problem she has. "You know more about it than anyone else," he says. "Will you advise her?"

What's Going on Here: Remaining on speaking terms with an ex is admirable. You like his mother and got along famously with her. Still, as much as you miss her, speaking with your mother-in-law only reminds you of the sorrowful breakup and the sadness you feel. You've moved on.

Response: "I can't. Talking to your mom brings back too many memories. I hope you understand."

Alert: When reminders are painful, it is time to cut your connection to an ex, including conversations with his or her parents.

··· SCENARIO ···

"My parents are staying two weeks this year.
That's not a problem for you, is it?"

What's Going on Here: One week seems more than reasonable to put up with any guest. Two weeks of in-laws, no matter how much you love them, can be emotionally taxing, in addition to preparing extra meals and being extra cordial when you come home from work. Here's the clincher: you get along better with your partner's parents than your partner does—they will be picking at each other within two days. So add umpire to your assignment list.

Response: "Have you lost your mind? No, they can't stay that long—and, yes, it's a huge problem."

Alert: It's your home, too, giving you the right to help decide who visits and for how long.

··· SCENARIO ···

"Really, you have to weed out some of these
books. They are taking over the house."

What's Going on Here: Your partner is an incurable neat freak and the clutter is getting to him. He sees your penchant for collecting as out of control.

Response: "I wouldn't know where to begin. I can't part with my books (I need all the tools, I love every piece of my collection)."

Alert: To you, the ever-growing collection you may have spent years amassing represents your life. You have a right to your treasures. If you stress their importance, maybe you and your partner can strike a compromise, keeping the items but organizing them in a better way.

··· SCENARIO ···

"Look at these puppies that Priya's dog had!" your partner says, showing you photos on her smartphone. "I want one. Four are already spoken for since she posted the photos this morning. Can we please get one?"

What's Going on Here: You're split on getting a dog. On one hand, you're both animal lovers, but only you seem to realize that you and your partner work twelve-hour days in offices that aren't dog friendly. Still, you know you'll eventually get a dog.

Response: "Our jobs are so constraining, and the dog would be alone too much. Let's wait until one of us has more flexibility or until we can afford a dog walker for the middle of the day."

Alert: Don't be afraid to inject realism about your circumstances into a *no*.

··· SCENARIO ···

"Will you feed Bandit?"

What's Going on Here: Isn't it enough that you feed the entire family every night? You made it clear when you got the dog that you would only feed two-legged creatures, that the rest of the family would feed the "family dog."

Response: "No, we had a deal."

Alert: The simple requests, the ones that you can accomplish in a few minutes, are thorny. Agree one night and feeding the dog may be on your permanent to-do list, along with cleaning the fish tank and doing the dishes.

··· SCENARIO ···

"We're almost finished—only four more boxes. Can't you take a break after we unpack the last ones?"

What's Going on Here: You've been unpacking for two days and your back hurts, your feet are swollen, your hands are sore, and you're hungry. If you don't sit down and rest for ten minutes, you may burst into tears.

Response: "I'm taking a break now."

Alert: Statements that say "This is what I'm doing" make it clear you're not looking for permission or approval. By not asking, it becomes clear that you can't be talked or argued out of what you want to do.

··· SCENARIO ···

"My parents are expecting us for Christmas week. Please make the travel arrangements."

What's Going on Here: You've spent every Christmas with his family for years—with pleasure. But you're tired of fighting the Christmas travel crowds with cranky kids in tow. It would be relaxing to be home in your own living room on Christmas morning, celebrating with your own friends during the holiday week.

Response: "Let's stay home this year. Invite your parents to come here."

Alert: Don't be wishy-washy about decisions that involve changes to expected rituals. Construct new ones—and have your partner, not you, tell his or her parents.

••• SCENARIO •••

"I want to watch the last play of the game. Will you put the chops on the grill?"

What's Going on Here: Every weekend, all weekend, he watches sports. Sporting events and games air round-the-clock. How can every game be so important that you find yourself preparing meals without help? Hint: you are allowing it.

Response: "Tell me what time you'll be ready. I'll wait."

Alert: Give yourself time to get your emotions in check before you answer. Once you make your point, he'll get the picture. Have a snack if you're hungry.

••• SCENARIO •••

"Please put those papers away and wipe the kitchen counters before our company arrives."

What's Going on Here: Your husband, wife, or partner has a fetish about messy counters and doesn't want company to see the kitchen in a state of disarray. No matter who creates the mess, you clean it up.

Response: "No, you can do that as well as I can. I have to get dressed."

Alert: Old "dogs" can perform new tricks if you ask.

··· SCENARIO ···

"There's a holiday office party for managers, spouses, and significant others. Will you come?"

What's Going on Here: All your insecurities may come rushing to the surface: What will I say to these people my partner works with? What will I wear? You would rather stay home. The stress of pulling yourself together and attending a function you find intimidating is too terrifying.

Response: "No, I really don't want to go."

Alert: It's unlikely that your absence will compromise your partner's job.

··· SCENARIO ···

"Can the guys come over later?" your partner texts. "We'll be quiet."

What's Going on Here: Your husband knows that if he were to ask you in person or on the phone, he'd get an immediate *no*. He's thinking you'll be too distracted to absorb his text message.

Response: "I prefer not. I would be unhappy if they did."

Alert: He's been warned.

··· SCENARIO ···

*"Will you organize the playroom
while I'm gone this week?"*

What's Going on Here: You know you can do it faster and better than anyone in your household, but organizing the playroom (or garage) should be a family project. Fight the urge to clean up, even if the disarray drives you crazy.

Response: "Not without everyone's help. We can all do it when you return from your business trip."

Alert: You're brainwashed. It is not easier to do it yourself, and beyond that, being compulsive is exhausting. Asking for help is a sign of maturity.

··· SCENARIO ···

*"I really think it's time to have a
baby," your husband says.*

What's Going on Here: You and your husband are both climbing the career ladder. You agreed to have children eventually, but he's been pressing the issue lately.

Response: "It's not time yet. Let's wait a year or two."

Alert: Not only is the number of women delaying having a first child until after age thirty growing in developed countries, but studies also indicate that younger first-time moms are at a career disadvantage. Waiting until after at least age thirty-one reduces the likelihood of lifetime income losses for women.

··· SCENARIO ···

"My parents are coming over for the afternoon,"
your spouse announces. "You said yourself that
they were helpful with the baby. Okay?"

What's Going on Here: The new baby arrived and so did your in-laws (and parents). Everyone's thrilled and wants to visit, and they have. You're exhausted.

Response: "Definitely not okay. We need time by ourselves to adjust to all the change. Tell them maybe in a few days."

Alert: In spite of your lifelong attachment to parents, loyalty should be to your partner or spouse. Respect her or his wishes.

··· SCENARIO ···

"Give me five minutes, I have to look at
this updated proposal," your wife says,
running to her laptop upstairs.

What's Going on Here: You put out popcorn and hot chocolate for the weekly family movie night when your spouse hears the familiar ding of incoming e-mail. She's knee-deep in a demanding project, but after working overtime all week, you hope she will reserve a couple hours for you and the kids.

Response: "We haven't seen you all week. It's the weekend—the proposal can wait until the movie is over. Can't it?"

Alert: Letting her know the family missed her during the week and that you want her with you keeps you from coming off as forbidding or belittling.

··· SCENARIO ···

*"I'm signing Rocky up for two extra
swim sessions," your wife tells you.*

What's Going on Here: Your wife was practically an Olympic swimmer (track star, gymnast, basketball player), and she is determined that your son will go to the Olympics to win the medal she never got.

Response: "Do you really think that's wise? I am completely against pushing him. He is going to turn away from the sport if you push him too hard."

Alert: This is right on. You cannot raise a child to be your clone or hope he or she will win the accolades you still covet.

... 4 ...

With Children— Park Your Guilt

I t doesn't matter if your children are toddlers, teens, or adults—they seem to always need or want something from you. And often, they want it "Now!" At times it can feel as if a child's needs and wants involve you in different and demanding ways every waking moment. "Drive me, buy me, let me, help me . . ." Most parents feel guilty when they're not able to make their child happy, and saying no only amplifies their guilt.

For many parents, the prospect of saying no feels wrong. Parents want to—and many persistently—say yes to their children to the detriment of themselves and their offspring. The inability to refuse a child has caused a widespread dramatic shift from parents being in charge to children orchestrating their parents' lives. We've become a culture of yes-parenting. As a result, parents end up feeling exhausted, stressed, and walked over, with their own needs pushed to the back burner.

Face it: life is more difficult when you always put your children ahead of yourself. Amid the thousands of regular tasks that constitute parenting, it can be challenging to step back and consider whether you are a yes-parent.

Quiz: How Much of a Yes-Parent Are You?

If your life resembles most of the items in the checklist below, it might be time to up your "no-how."

1. At least one room in your home looks like a toy or computer store.
2. You know the first names and personal details of the servers at your son's favorite restaurant.
3. Your living room is more often a place for wrestling, hide-and-seek, or arts and crafts than for adult conversation or relaxing.
4. Your daughter's sweet-sixteen celebration was almost as extravagant as your wedding.
5. You spend Saturday evenings driving your children and their friends from place to place.
6. Your eight-year-old stays up so late that he can recite *The Tonight Show* monologue.
7. Your teen's smartphone data charges are higher than the amount of money you spent on your own wardrobe in the last year.
8. Your child has every outfit, toy, and gadget that her best friend owns.
9. You have three dogs, two kittens, and a goldfish—and somehow you've become the family dog walker, litter box emptier, and fishbowl cleaner.
10. Your adult child recently borrowed money to buy a new car, to put a deposit on an apartment, or to invest in a friend's business.

If your yeses outweigh your nos, it's likely you need to do more limit setting. Parenting is a forever proposition. You'll be saying no—or should be—for decades, so park your guilt.

When your children reach adulthood, they will find something other than your refusals to fault you for.

Some would argue that pleasing their children makes them happy, and that's fine to a certain extent. However, saying no opens a door to freedom for parents to feel less depleted and enjoy their children more. No is about fewer hassles and arguments . . . and ultimately, about raising caring, responsible, respectful children. Your children may even thank you one day for what they learned from your *no* responses.

Why Parents Say Yes

Saying no to children sometimes means ignoring the inclination to raise "star" children—a tendency that is prevalent today. Saying no is about letting go of the desire to keep up with friends, relatives, and neighbors. Sometimes it can feel as if every other parent you know is saying yes and you are the only holdout. (Your kids will try to make you feel that way, too.) Deciphering your own motives can help break a permissive *yes* cycle and free you to take a different approach going forward.

Sometimes we think we are depriving our children of something desperately desired—a toy, time with friends, a monetary loan. We feel guilty, but we shouldn't. Taking a look at what motivates your decision-making as a parent can put you more at ease saying no. Get over the guilt that yours will be the only child who didn't get a soccer trophy, attend a party, or visit the new amusement park.

Why you may be a yes-parent:

- To relieve a sense of guilt for spending limited time with your children
- To replicate the indulgences and advantages your parents gave you

- To counter practices and approaches your parents used
- To make up for things you didn't have in your own childhood
- To be popular with your children, to win them over, or to gain their approval
- To keep peace—because you can't bear to see your child unhappy for a single second

Before you agree to what a child asks, think back: Is your yes response a reaction to what may have happened to you as a youngster, or is your agreement or denial what you want to do as a parent now?

The Benefits of No-Parenting

Parents hope to operate in a middle ground, to be strong guides and still be warm and loving, authoritative rather than authoritarian. You don't have to be a yes-parent—nor do you want your children to fear you. The desired equilibrium is one in which parents remain in charge while saying no respectfully, in a way that is not threatening or shaming. There is no universal standard for being an exemplary parent. You will make mistakes. But, you decide what you feel will be most developmentally helpful for your child while giving him room to make choices.

Children may see your denials as not being supportive. Clearly, that is not the case. You don't want to break your children's spirit or enthusiasm, but you want them to recognize and respect boundaries. Your decisions instill and reinforce your values and beliefs.

Many parental nos are actually learning opportunities for children. Strategic nos reduce the chance that a child of any age will feel entitled, believe that everything is coming her way. Among other positives, refusals help children learn to cope with disappointment, become resilient, and sharpen their decision-making ability. These are skills they will need later in life. Once you realize how beneficial a *no* can be for both of you, you will probably use it more frequently.

There will be times, especially as children get older, when no-parenting could and should involve a *yes* or a negotiation. Agree with your child or make an exception when the request is reasonable or he least expects it. An occasional or surprising *yes* helps soften what can be experienced as an endless stream of *no*.

Before you give in, think about the details of what's really involved. Will saying yes lead to more time driving in traffic, more money spent, bigger messes to clean up, or later bedtimes that could result in having a tired, difficult child the next day?

Training Ground: The Early Years

With very young children, most parents face unattractive, challenging behavior from time to time: whining, back talk, tantrums, or aggression. Young children misbehave to test your love and limits; it's what they do. Untoward actions require parents to step in for safety reasons, to clarify restrictions or suggest alternatives as a way to teach children what is acceptable and what has to stop.

A combination of standing strong and comforting very young children helps them cope with feelings and situations that are beyond their grasp. The word *no* doesn't work a lot of the time, but you will want to keep trying. Think of the early years as a training ground for socialization and setting the stage for peaceful coexistence in the coming years.

Setting limits gives children behavioral guidelines and tools that transfer to spheres beyond home. That fact alone should spur you to keep trying. Along the way, call up your sense of humor and an extra dollop of patience. You will need both. Incidents you found so disturbing when your child was a toddler likely will be laughed about years later. Here are some difficulties you may face and ways to address them, along with insight into how restrictions and denials benefit children.

··· SCENARIO ···

You find your son in the kitchen, surrounded by bits of an expensive bowl that you explicitly told him to never touch. "I didn't do it!" he yells and then tries to run away.

What's Going on Here: You are furious. Your child smashed one of your favorite possessions. Your inclination is to berate him. Pause so you can react as mildly as possible.

Response: "I'm very unhappy that the bowl was broken. I am sure you feel bad, and I know you didn't mean to break it. I love you, but I won't allow you to throw things—especially things you were told not to touch."

Alert: It is okay to let a child know that you are angry or frustrated by the outcome or potential outcome of his actions. It's most important that you distinguish between the event and the child, reassuring him that while you don't like what happened, you still love him.

··· SCENARIO ···

"Send her back. I don't want to keep her,"
your three-year-old tells you. She's wildly
stamping her feet and pointing a finger
dangerously close to her baby sister's eyes.

What's Going on Here: Your older child is reasonably dismayed; she's been dethroned. You thought you prepared her well for the arrival of a sibling, yet you face unadulterated misery, jealousy, and disdain you never expected.

Response: "You can tell me you are upset, but you have to promise to be very careful around the baby. The baby isn't going anywhere; she is part of our family. Having a sister doesn't change how much we love you. We have plenty of hugs and kisses and love for both of you. Come here, I'll show you."

Alert: Your daughter reveals her strong feelings of being displaced. She feels unloved or loved less than the new arrival. Spending more one-on-one time with your older child, giving her "real" tasks to demonstrate that the baby needs her, and reassuring her that you love her will help to ease a lot of her fears and unhappiness. Compliment her efforts at being a good big sister to someone so that your toddler overhears you.

··· SCENARIO ···

"Feed me, too. You always feed the baby and you
don't feed me anymore," your toddler whines.

What's Going on Here: An older child's asking to be fed, wanting a bottle, reverting to bed-wetting, or having "accidents" is not unusual when you attend to a younger sibling who actually needs you to do things he can't do for himself. Older children think they are being overlooked. Reassure your child that this won't go on forever.

Response: "Honey, do you remember when I fed you? I did and we had fun" (talk about a funny incident if you recall one). Or, "It's great that I don't have to feed you anymore. That tells me you are big boy and we are very proud of you. I can't feed both of you at the same time. Soon your sister will be a big girl and be able to do all the things you can do yourself. Will you help me teach her?"

Alert: When an older child shows signs of regressing, it's time for parents to give him more attention in other ways (read an extra book at bedtime or talk about special privileges he has because he's older). This tells him he has a special place in the family.

··· SCENARIO ···

*"But I'm clean. I didn't do anything messy today.
No bath for Benny," your child tells you.*

What's Going on Here: Your young one has decided that he has the final say. Not quite.

Response: "I know you feel clean. You even look almost clean, but you are not shining clean. Let's pretend you played in mud all day and we are going to transform you into a star that twinkles brightly in the sky. Can you do that?"

Alert: Bathing and teeth-brushing routines around bedtime help children feel secure and keep the household from lapsing into free-for-alls of urging and insisting by parents. Down the road, early nightly routines help instill good hygiene habits.

··· SCENARIO ···

"You promised we would go to the zoo today. You lied to me!" Your four-year-old flails his arms and punches you.

What's Going on Here: Your first reaction is to grab your son's arms to stop him. You are appalled by the way he handles his frustration. If possible, walk away until you can curb your own emotions. Then get down to your child's eye level to talk to him, put him on your lap, or put your arms around him to comfort him. Not always possible, but worth trying.

Response: "I know you are very unhappy, but hitting (or kicking) won't change anything. Let's come up with some better ways for you to show how angry you are."

Alert: Most young children don't know what to do when they are feeling strong emotions. Tell your child that it is okay to be angry. Give your young child alternatives to hitting: yelling, counting to ten, stomping his feet. Practice with him and remind him that hitting is not allowed. Hitting hurts whether it's mom, dad, sister, brother, or a friend who distresses you.

··· SCENARIO ···

"It's my toy! Mom gave it to me," your younger child shrieks.

"She did not. She gave it to both of us and said we had to share," your older child yells while pulling hard on the toy.

What's Going on Here: Fighting over toys is a common conflict whenever siblings are playing together, more so when they are close in age. Each child wants to claim ownership and looks to a parent to say so. It almost doesn't make any difference to whom the toy belongs . . . and you may not even recall who is its rightful owner.

Response: "If you can't figure out how to share it, I will take it away. That's final. What do you want to do?"

Alert: Your children can have a toy chest bursting with toys. Nonetheless, they will probably want whatever their sister or brother has at that moment. Encouraging them to work it out helps them develop conflict resolution skills they will surely need with their peers. Typically, the ability to share is not fully developed until age three or four.

··· SCENARIO ···

You tell your four-year-old it's time to leave the playground. "I'm NOT leaving!!!!" he screams, throwing himself on the ground.

What's Going on Here: When a child is happily engaged in an activity, the thought of stopping feels unreasonable. He is angry and that feeling, like other emotions, should be acknowledged.

Response: "I know you are angry, but it's time to go. Let's make a plan to come back soon."

Alert: It's tempting to give in when your child is screaming and you feel judged by the other adults within earshot, but resist the temptation. Without being stopped, your child will come to learn he can tyrannize and bully you. Although his endeavor at bossy behavior is unacceptable, you want to name what he is feeling so he can learn to interpret his emotions.

··· SCENARIO ···

"I'm not eating that," your child says with a turned-up nose, as if you placed the dog's kibble in front of him.

What's Going on Here: Many young children are picky eaters. Knowing that, you put *some* foods on his plate that he likes and will probably eat. But he doesn't appreciate your efforts.

Response: "I understand you are not pleased with what I'm serving. Eat what you want, but that's dinner tonight."

Alert: Children don't usually starve themselves, so toughen up to disapproval of your meal selection or cooking. If you comply and make something different after every complaint or for everyone in the family, you might as well be a professional line cook.

··· SCENARIO ···

"Reid threw sand in my eyes!" your child's buddy screams.

What's Going on Here: The children were quietly building castles in the sandbox or on the beach. Your son tries to explain that his friend started it by saying mean things.

Response: "I don't care who started it. We don't throw sand at people. How would you feel if someone threw sand in your eyes?"

Alert: Empathy can be learned early by asking your child to put himself in the other person's shoes. Preschoolers and young toddlers understand that other people have feelings. Underscore the lesson by asking children how they would feel if they were the person being harmed.

··· **SCENARIO** ···

"That's a stupid game. You're stupid. If you won't build towers, I'm not playing with you anymore,"
you overhear your child arguing with a friend.

What's Going on Here: Children can be so mean to each other. When a dispute or name-calling escalates to the point of a possible free-for-all, a parent needs to step in.

Response: "Stop shouting, you two. I get it. One of you wants to build towers, and the other wants to play the game."

Alert: Young children have difficulty grasping that someone else has different wants. Once you acknowledge both children's desires, propose choices such as number of minutes doing what one child wants and the same amount of time for the other's preference. If that fails, take time out for a snack or go outside to remove the children from the situation entirely.

··· SCENARIO ···

"You said you would play a board game with me before dinner. Come on, I have it all set up."

What's Going on Here: Not realizing all you had to do, you agreed to play a game, but preparing dinner is taking longer than you expected.

Response: "Honey, I know you want to play, but I have to finish making dinner first. You will have to be patient. If we don't play before dinner, we can after dinner or tomorrow."

Alert: It's a good time to ask your child to help out with dinner in some small ways, setting the table or handing you ingredients. Whether or not they work outside the home, parents often feel guilty for not spending what they consider enough time with their children, even though parents today spend almost twice as much time with their kids as parents did in the mid-1960s.

··· SCENARIO ···

"Time's up," you tell your child. "Give it to me." You are shocked by the intensity and volume of the screams and her tight grip on the video game device.

What's Going on Here: Your youngster thinks that if she is obnoxious long enough she will get to play longer. Give in and you run the risk of setting a precedent that she can be successful in getting what she wants if she resists hard and long enough.

Response: "Listen to me. If you don't give it to me in ten seconds you won't have it at all tomorrow."

Alert: The research is clear that screen time over-stimulates children's developing brains and nervous system. Allowing extended video game play for young children actually increases their stress levels and sets them up for meltdowns. It may help to give a young child a five-minute warning that time is almost up.

··· SCENARIO ···

*"I'm not going to school and you can't make me,"
your (almost) kindergartner announces as the
reality of going to school looms large in her mind.*

What's Going on Here: The start of school in the fall, a new school, or going back after a lengthy vacation sets off alarm bells for some children. The source of a child's anxiety ranges from the idea of leaving the security of a parent's presence to peer problems or academic pressure.

Response: "I know you can handle it. I'm sure of that. You are going to surprise yourself."

Alert: Repeated doses of reassurance and encouragement should help in situations that create anxiety in children. Don't underscore anxiety by asking for specifics: Are you afraid no one will eat lunch with you? Or, are you worried the kids will tease you? Reassuring your child that she can handle a situation (be it a test, party, sport activity) will help allay some of the fear.

· · · · · · · · · · · ·

Elementary Rules: Using *No* with School-Aged Children

Parents want to build on the groundwork they started when their children were younger. As children become involved at school and socially, being a mom or dad becomes more complicated. It can feel as if every parent is trying to give his or her child an advantage in one arena or another—sports, academics, the arts . . . During the elementary school years, the pressure to keep up with the Joneses and raise "star" children intensifies.

With or without pressure, constantly acquiescing places a needless burden on you. More *no* answers mean less exhaustion and the reduced likelihood that you are operating on a short fuse. By saying no when appropriate, you can get off the yes-treadmill and avoid your children taking control. When leaning toward a *yes*—but knowing it should be a *no*—rethink why you may be choosing that route.

More importantly, requests you make that children try to ignore or refuse are the very ones parents should insist upon. The Harvard Grant Study tracked graduates from 1938 on and showed a positive correlation between chores and success in adulthood. Be reasonable, but be firm . . . and the earlier you begin chores—having your young children put away toys or put their clothes in the hamper—the better off your kids will be in the long term. In sum, chores are one of the biggest factors in shoring up a work ethic and preparing children for success.

Sometimes kids make the most outrageous or time-consuming requests, while other "asks" go against your values or better judgment. It's a parent's job to enforce boundaries calmly no matter how emotional a child becomes when he thinks he's right or justified. Keep in mind that how you say no often determines how effective your *no* will be. Yelling doesn't work. Sometimes you need to lower your voice for children to hear you. Skip the lectures whenever possible.

To complicate matters, the universal presence of technology in its many forms and the increased use of computers and tablets in schools add another layer of potential conflict and can leave a parent unsure about what parameters or constraints to put in place. It can be oh so tempting, with children's hectic schedules, to give in or let them stay glued to their devices.

··· SCENARIO ···

"You have to wash my soccer uniform now."

What's Going on Here: Your child either forgot to tell you he had a game or forgot to throw his mud-spattered shorts and socks into the hamper earlier.

Response: "No, but I'll show you how to use the washer and dryer."

Alert: Teaching children laundry basics at an early age will make you feel less like the laundress—and your children feel more competent and confident.

··· SCENARIO ···

"I am not going to play with him! My little brother is no fun," your older child argues.

What's Going on Here: Your daughter is not keen on playing with her younger brother and balks repeatedly. You need her to entertain him for a short period so you can send a few important e-mails, clean up, etc.

Response: "Please do it for me. I am almost finished, and then I will take you and your brother to the park. Maybe one of your friends will be there. We could call Jordan or Jessica later to find out."

Alert: Children don't see the same prestige in playing with a sibling as they do in playing with a friend. Appealing to children's desire to please their parents can work. You are trying to foster a close relationship between your children, whatever their genders, but so often that takes maturity. Ideally a warm friendship will evolve at some point.

··· SCENARIO ···

"It's not fair: I want to go to bed when Katie does. It doesn't matter if she's older than me!"

What's Going on Here: School-age children are very concerned about "fairness" and not having to go to bed earlier than their friends or siblings. From a child's point of view, you are giving an older child preferential treatment with a later bedtime. He'll fight you on this one.

Response: "No. You need the extra sleep to help you grow. When you are Katie's age, you can stay up later."

Alert: It's wise to be the boss of your young children when something like sleep affects their health and development. The National Sleep Foundation recommends elementary school children get eight to eleven hours of sleep a day. Consider this solid ammunition for standing your ground.

··· SCENARIO ···

*"I can handle the new serial killer movie,"
your ten-year-old declares. "I won't be
scared, and all my friends are going."*

What's Going on Here: Your daughter is confident and is being honest with you, but you certainly won't let her see such a frightening and violent slasher flick. You're worried that if you give a hard *no*, she'll resent you and find a way to watch it anyway.

Response: "I really don't think you realize what you're getting yourself into. Worst-case scenario, you won't sleep for nights afterward or embarrass yourself in front of your friends by how scared you get. How about you hang out with your friends after the movie?"

Alert: Your daughter doesn't realize the impact that seeing such a movie will have on her. You do.

··· SCENARIO ···

*Your children beg, "Can we get a dog?"
They pledge to take care of him.*

What's Going on Here: In theory, the children mean what they say. They think they will attend to the new pet, but as parent, you'll be doing 95 percent of the caretaking no matter what they promise. Don't agree unless you would like a dog yourself.

Response: "No." Then, add all your practical reasons for the decision: "We work, everyone's schedule is full, we don't have sufficient yard space, someone in the family is allergic . . ."

Alert: While the dog may not require frequent walks in his youth, the dog could need out six or seven times a day when older, about the time your children are off to college.

··· SCENARIO ···

"I want a cell phone," your eight-year-old claims. "Jade and Will have one. I won't ask for anything else," he adds, thinking that will convince you.

What's Going on Here: Your child hopes that if you know his best friends have cell phones, you will be more likely to be swayed into agreement.

Response: "I know it seems like all your friends have phones. Really, I don't think they do. We will get you a phone, but not yet."

Alert: In some situations, such as a child who walks to and from school, has parents who share custody, or is home alone after school, a cell phone may be a reasonable idea for an eight-year-old. Generally, only older children in their tweens and teens are mature enough to handle the responsibility and understand and follow their parents' cell phone rules.

··· SCENARIO ···

"Dad, please help me with my homework," your sixth grader asks.

What's Going on Here: Homework "help" too frequently translates to a parent doing the assignment. Encouraging your child to do his own work builds confidence.

Response: "I am sure you can do it yourself. I have every faith in your ability."

Alert: Teachers want to know what children have mastered and where they may need direction or extra help. No matter how you camouflage the project, math sheet, or essay, your child's teacher will be able to spot your contribution, be it in concept, the finished product, or perfect answers. For that reason alone, encourage academic independence.

··· SCENARIO ···

"The coach wants one of you to be his assistant. Please, will you do it?"

What's Going on Here: You hate to disappoint your child, but the reality is you can barely make it to the games on a regular basis because you are driving your other child to her extra-curricular activities (and possibly bundling the baby into the car, too). Being required to be on the field for every practice and game means finding someone else to drive your younger daughter and/or to babysit.

Response: "Honey, I would love to do that, but it's not possible."

Alert: Children get over disappointment far more easily and faster than parents do. They are more resilient than you probably realize.

··· SCENARIO ···

*"Can I rake the leaves later, Dad?" Substitute
most anything you ask your children to do: set the
table, do the dishes, sweep the porch, mow the
lawn, pull the weeds, water the garden, take out
the garbage. The operative word here is* later.

What's Going on Here: Asking for a postponement is a stall. Your child hopes you'll forget about the chore or, better yet, get aggravated and do it yourself. He's banking on one or the other happening.

Response: "No."

Alert: Children are specialists in avoiding chores that smack of work. In a busy parent's life, your child comes out the winner if you agree to any form of procrastination. Have them do tasks when asked, no negotiation.

··· SCENARIO ···

*"Dad, can you go on the class trip to the
museum? It will be so fun! Please be a
chaperone, please," your child begs.*

What's Going on Here: You are a working parent, and taking a day off for your child's trip is not an option. You feel guilty about how often you miss opportunities to spend time with your child that are important to him.

Response: "You know I would love to go to the museum. Honey, I have to go to work. I know you are disappointed; so am I."

Alert: Don't confuse being sad with feeling guilty that you can't be a chaperone. Reserve feeling guilty for the instances when you have done something you are sorry about or believe you shouldn't have done—losing your temper at your child because you had a bad day at the office, for example.

··· SCENARIO ···

"Can I invite my science team for dinner tonight? We need to decide what we want to do for our final project," your eleven-year-old asks.

What's Going on Here: Your daughter is a leader and enthusiastic about her studies. All good. You want to acknowledge her diligence, but not when her requests are going to throw your week into chaos or give you extra work.

Response: "That's five people, right? Let's talk about having them over when it's not a school night for you and a work night for me. That way you can help me, and you will have more time to talk about your project."

Alert: Brokering a sensible solution avoids a hard *no* and in this instance gives your child some responsibility for feeding her friends.

··· SCENARIO ···

"I'm going to baseball camp. I don't care what you say. I REALLY, REALLY want to go," your twelve-year-old announces.

What's Going on Here: Your son is a stellar pitcher; he played on a local and travel team this season. He was largely responsible for his team's local and statewide wins. You're a proud parent and admire his passion and devotion to the game, but he needs to give his arm a rest.

Response: "We know you really want to go. We support you, but we have to say baseball camp is not happening this summer. We'll find something else you like."

Alert: By saying no to excessive participation, you avoid possible injury and extreme fatigue. The American Academy of Pediatrics finds that young and adolescent participants who play a variety of sports have fewer injuries and play sports longer than those who specialize in one sport before puberty.

··· SCENARIO ···

*"Dad, Danny is twisting my arm. Ouch,
you're hurting me, Danny. Stop it!"
one of your children bellows.*

What's Going on Here: You hear a bloodcurdling scream from the room in which you thought your two children were playing amicably. Your knee-jerk reaction is to run in and rescue "the victim."

Response: "In our family, we don't hurt each other. We take care of each other. Do you understand?"

Alert: It's clear to you who is at fault, but a blanket "not in our family" response delivers a message that doesn't single out or shame the perpetrator. It tells both children what is acceptable.

··· SCENARIO ···

*"But, Mom said I could go to the museum
with Bharath's family this afternoon."*

What's Going on Here: Your son often uses the "But, Mom said" approach when he doesn't like your answer. You're always inclined to agree as an automatic reaction, deferring to what your wife said.

Response: "You didn't finish your chores, and I don't think Mom realizes that. I will talk to her, but for right now, you may not go with Bharath."

Alert: Children learn how to divide and conquer at tender ages. You can avoid a lot of conflict within the family if you and your partner are on the same page about what is permissible and what rules are ironclad.

··· SCENARIO ···

*"Mom, we'll be fine. You can let us stay home
alone while you have lunch with your friend."*

What's Going on Here: News reports of parents being arrested and charged with negligence have changed how we allow children freedoms and give them responsibility. Your ten-year-old wants to prove she is competent, that she can take good care of herself and her younger sibling, but you worry. Your first thought is to refuse your child's request. Leaving children home alone is taboo.

Response: "Yes, but only for a short amount of time, and you must abide by these rules . . ." Your child is ecstatic.

Alert: When a youngster asks to take on responsibility, it is wise to allow it if the circumstances seem safe and reasonable. The odds that something will happen are slim. You may be more worried about how people will judge you than the risk involved. This is one instance in which you want to consider changing an emphatic *no* to a *yes* and provide parameters for what she is to do with her younger sibling.

⋯ SCENARIO ⋯

"You said when I got older, I could have a TV in my room. On my birthday I will hit double digits," your nine-year-old reminds you.

What's Going on Here: Since you said that, you have learned that children with TVs in their rooms do not do as well academically, are more prone to weight gain, and may develop sleep problems caused by the screen's blue light.

Response: "I remember saying that, but I changed my mind. I know you are not happy, but the same rules we have for your smartphone would apply to a TV."

Alert: Parents, you're allowed to change your mind. The issues created by TV in children's bedrooms apply to tablets and cell phones on which children can play games and watch endless videos and movies. For children, device use at bedtime doubles the chances of poor sleep.

··· SCENARIO ···

*Out to dinner, your daughter finished
her soda before the meals arrive. "Can I
please have another soda?" she asks.*

What's Going on Here: You have a firm policy with your children about sugary drinks when the family eats in restaurants: only one soda. You may be inclined to order her a second drink to keep your child happy in public.

Response: "You know our policy. I will get you a glass of water."

Alert: Be sure your dining-out rules and limits are clear and understood by your children. Giving in sets you up for repeated pleas and pestering because your children come to expect that you will break your own rules—something you do only on special occasions or as a surprise treat now and then.

··· SCENARIO ···

*"Mr. Petrosian thinks I should apply for the
summer STEM program," your fifth grader
announces, referring to her science teacher.
"Can I? Everyone at school is saying how it
would look great on a college application."*

What's Going on Here: You knew your daughter's new school was more competitive than other grade schools out there, but this talk of college applications when she's years from entering high school throws you. She is bright and ambitious, but the program would require her going away for weeks. It seems more than she can handle at this age.

Response: "I'm so thrilled that he thinks you're a great candidate! But we need to talk about this huge commitment. The program seems very intense. Let's look at our options, maybe there is a comparable program that will be as exciting but is closer to home and not as rigorous."

Alert: Children recognize and are affected by pressure, leading some to rebel. Others, like this young lady, jump on the bandwagon. For parents, the pressure to have a child excel or succeed begins early. Some parents start résumé building to give their child a leg up (hoping their child will attend a prestigious college or get a sports or academic scholarship, for example). Don't get caught up in the frenzy.

. . . .

Patient Parenting: The Teen Years

Your younger children looked to you for answers or assistance more often than not. That made you feel needed and loved. Then everything changed. The high approval rating you once proudly owned vanished in a flash. We would all like some signs that tweens and teens approve of us, but as they get older and become more independent, you might want to resign yourself to waiting for that time to return. Be patient, but above all, be a parent.

During the teen years, saying no becomes more difficult—and more essential—as adolescents push their parents. The policies you had in place during their younger years will be tested as teens grapple with their identity and struggle for independence.

You may remember what a struggle you had: trying to fit in, act grown up, and forge your own personality, but having parents who seemed to stifle your attempts. Disagreeing with your parents' decisions and possibly breaking the rules now and then defined those years. Being angry when you were told no to going to a party or being grounded for not respecting a sibling—that was your norm. Your teen is more than likely to feel and act the same way.

Being a parent of an adolescent is not about winning a popularity contest. It is about providing solid guidance. Frequently that involves saying no to keep your teen on track to becoming a caring and responsible citizen. Steel yourself, because teens want to make their own choices even when you are convinced their decisions are risky.

At any point, parents can slip into a yes-mode because teenagers are adept at crushing parents' resolve. They have the language proficiency to make earnest, plausible cases for what they want, and their moody, obstreperous behavior can wear you down. Sticking with no-parenting reduces the chances of feeling coerced or manipulated by your children. However, on occasion you will want to back off or present alternatives that might work *and* achieve the desired outcome (or at least come close). That is not giving in; that's smart parenting.

··· SCENARIO ···

"Can I wear makeup? I'm a teenager now."

What's Going on Here: Your teenager thinks lipstick, blush, eyeliner, and mascara will enhance her looks. You're appalled at her being a painted lady at age thirteen. Yet, you've noticed her friends have begun to wear makeup.

Response: "That's not an idea I'm overjoyed by. My overall reaction is no, but let's talk about it."

Alert: You're bucking peer pressure, and your teen will think you are being unreasonable if you flat-out refuse. View her asking as an opportunity to influence her makeup choices and to teach her the proper way, as you see it, to apply cosmetics. Consider giving her the go-ahead with limitations you feel appropriate—not to school, not to family functions, not on occasions that make you uncomfortable.

··· SCENARIO ···

"It's not fair. All the other kids have at least two pairs (tons) of those sneakers. I get a measly one!" your son pouts.

What's Going on Here: You and your teenager are shopping for school clothes, and he wants items you think are superfluous or too expensive.

Response: "You can have one or the other. Put the other one on your birthday or holiday list. I'm guessing someone in the family will buy it for you."

Alert: Teens want to make the latest fashion statement, be it sneakers, jackets, or backpacks. To help alleviate shopping disagreements, give your child a budget. If he is shopping alone or with friends, a limited-amount credit card or allowance for the year helps restrain indulgences.

··· SCENARIO ···

"I had a tough week at school. All those tests. I'm skipping the SAT prep course tomorrow."

What's Going on Here: Your daughter is stressed for good reason and thinks she can play on your sympathy. She's successfully used this ploy before to get out of commitments.

Response: "I know you stayed up late almost every night studying, but you asked us to sign you up. Prep courses are expensive and you begged us. You can go to bed early and find the energy. You can't miss a review session."

Alert: Children, especially teens and preteens, agree to many things and then try to squirm out of their obligations or promises. Empathizing lets your child know you hear her, but at the same time saying no helps teach children the value of money.

••• SCENARIO •••

"I don't have too much homework. I'll do it when I get back from the skate park."

What's Going on Here: His concept of "a little homework" and yours may be—and often are—worlds apart.

Response: "No."

Alert: A strong *no* said while looking your teen right in the eye sets limits and underscores that you mean what you say. Parents' nos are sound lessons in how the world works—you don't always get what you want.

··· SCENARIO ···

"I'm not going to Grandpa Larry's birthday party. No one my age will be there," your teen announces, with hands on her hips for emphasis.

What's Going on Here: You may wonder what happened to your sweet, cooperative child. Couple that with garden-variety teen rebellion and you will see that she's seeking independence. Do not hold yourself responsible for your teen's or preteen's attempt to override you and ignore family obligations.

Response: "Of course you are going. We said we would be there, and we are going as a family. This party is not optional."

Alert: If you don't stand up to this bullying behavior, you are undermining the importance of keeping commitments and valuing family.

··· SCENARIO ···

"My room is almost clean. I will finish when I get home from meeting my friends for lunch," your teen promises.

What's Going on Here: You have been after your child to clean her pigpen of a room for weeks. She relentlessly pushes to meet her friends on weekends, and her promises go out the window once she gets her way.

Response: "That's not happening today. You have another hour or so of work on that room."

Alert: Be mindful: Teens will try a mix of promises, manipulations, and persistent badgering to have their way.

··· SCENARIO ···

"Can you hand me my phone?" your son asks while you're all packing up for a family day at the beach. "I want to get to the next level on my game."

What's Going on Here: You planned a family outing for everyone, including yourself, to unplug.

Response: "Today is a tech-free family day. It's very important to me that we step away from screens and spend time together. That can't happen when you're focused on beating your game, your sister's on Tumblr, or I'm texting."

Alert: Technology removes the magic from meaningful, in-person experiences, especially when spending precious time as a family. Screens offer distractions. Your children may bristle at not being able to play on their phones or tablets, but if you prioritize taking time to be in the moment with family, your children will take your cues and hopefully build healthy habits as they mature.

··· SCENARIO ···

"I suppose you're going to make me stay home and work on my paper when Cousin Beth visits." Your teen presents what sounds like a question but is more like an admission of guilt.

What's Going on Here: Your child has a project due on Monday, and her favorite cousin is visiting for the weekend. This isn't her first time-management failure. She's aware she should have started days ago. You wonder why she waited. You can insist she give up time with her cousin, or your response can let her know she can be master of her own "fate."

Response: "I know you want to spend as much time as you can with your cousin. How do you plan to get the project completed by Monday?"

Alert: Sometimes parents need to be flexible, to allow children to come up with solutions that get the "job" done. When asked for their input, teens are more likely to feel—and eventually become—responsible instead of prodded and controlled by their parents.

··· SCENARIO ···

"Dad, you're so conservative. All the girls are wearing short shorts and crop tops. It's normal."

What's Going on Here: You cringe at the thought of your teenager attending a school dance or any social gathering in the outfit she has on. You think it shouldn't leave her bedroom. You thought you were fairly liberal, but in your opinion this outfit is way too revealing.

Response: "I know you think what you have on is attractive, and it may be what all the girls are wearing, but I can't let you go out dressed like that."

Alert: It's fine for teens to argue with parents, to push back as they "try on" new identities. Pick and choose your battles carefully. Be leery of giving in to avoid an argument.

··· SCENARIO ···

"Mom, can I stay out an hour later tonight?
Jamie, Allie, and Erin's parents said yes."

What's Going on Here: You are responsible for the safety of this teenager who is pressuring you to change her curfew and alter what you believe is a good parenting practice. It's tempting to give in, but don't budge. Soften your *no* with concern.

Response: "No. I'll worry about you too much if you are out so late."

Alert: Guaranteed, your child will keep hounding, but she will find something much more unusual than enforcing a curfew to complain about.

··· SCENARIO ···

"Can I spend the night at Tommy's?"

What's Going on Here: Your son wants to spend the night at a friend's house, but you have only met Tommy once and his parents never. That's sufficient to prompt your answer.

Response: "No, your friend can sleep here if he likes." If your child pleads, add, "What part of no don't you understand?"

Alert: Follow your internal warnings. Parents don't always have to justify their nos. It's your prerogative to be adamant, even testy. File under "parental right."

··· SCENARIO ···

"You have to drive me to Andrew's house. It's very necessary," your adolescent implores. His asking fluctuates between whining and hysteria when you won't change your mind.

What's Going on Here: Few can make a situation appear more critical than the teen who wants to be with his friends to discuss the history assignment or the latest gossip. The begging makes missing either sound like a catastrophe.

Response: "I can't take you anywhere this afternoon. Between instant messaging, video chats, and phone calls, you can be connected enough to cope with this 'emergency.'"

Alert: Within half an hour, most teens will be content to use the gadgets they have at hand to fret over or work out the drama of the moment with their friends.

··· SCENARIO ···

"My guidance counselor said I can take four honors classes in the fall. Isn't that great?"

What's Going on Here: You have a classic overachiever, an honor student. Her academic prowess started in elementary school and hasn't stopped. She is motivated and driven—all good. Now that she's entering her last year of high school, you are worried about her health.

Response: "That's wonderful. We are very proud of you, but I'm not sure you need all four for college. We are also concerned about your being exhausted all the time. Do you remember how tired you were and how many times you were sick last year?"

Alert: Every child is different; some thrive on the overload and handle it without consequence. Others, like this young lady, don't. In such cases, parents need to take charge. Say no to open a negotiation about lightening her academic load and avoiding serious health problems.

··· SCENARIO ···

"You are so not being fair. I hate you! You make my life so miserable, Dad." Your teenaged son slams the door behind him and sulks in his room.

What's Going on Here: Your son wants to take a girl out on a date, but you believe he's too young. It breaks the rule you made clear a few years ago that he is not allowed to date until he is sixteen.

Response: "I am sorry you feel that way. I realize how important this girl is to you, but making sure you are mature enough and ready for dating is my responsibility. When you are a parent, you will be able to make the rules."

Alert: Parents are safe targets for teen outbursts. Since teenagers recognize parents and siblings as constants in their lives, they believe they can be rude or belligerent—approaches they would not dare try with friends or other adults.

··· SCENARIO ···

"My phone is not at the table," your teen insists, her foot on top of it so she can feel it vibrate. "It's on the floor under my chair."

What's Going on Here: You "get" that the phone is an extension of a teen's very being, a way to keep in touch with friends constantly. Yet you want your children to remember that you don't live in a hole; most of the time you know when they are trying to fool you.

Response: "I know where it is. Put your phone in the other room with everyone else's."

Alert: As a family, create a list of tech rules everyone must follow. Giving children some say in rule making around their devices increases the likelihood that the rules will be followed. Enforcing your family's tech rules ensures that your children interact with you and siblings. Face-to-face human interaction is essential for development at all ages.

··· SCENARIO ···

"Kara's parents let us have beer when we are at her house. Please? Kara and I will share one," your teenager asks before her friend arrives.

What's Going on Here: Your teen is on the cusp of adulthood and testing the limits. Other parents may allow their teenagers to drink at home as long as they are not driving, but that doesn't mean you have to follow suit.

Response: "I have no say in what Kara's parents do, but I will not serve alcohol to your friends who are still minors."

Alert: Feel good that your teenager is being straightforward with you. Don't overreact to learning she drinks beer at her friend's home, but be clear. Restate your feelings about alcohol and drug use. Teen brains are still developing, and they need parents' supervision to avoid risky behaviors.

··· SCENARIO ···

*"Dad, I can't pay those data charges.
You're joking, right?"*

What's Going on Here: You have a family data plan, and you warned your teen well in advance that he was dangerously close to using up his allotted data. You told him that he would have to pay the extra charges with money he earned during the summer.

Response: "No, I am not kidding. You had ample notice, and you chose to ignore it."

Alert: Holding teens accountable is good money-management training.

··· SCENARIO ···

"I'm going to pick up Doug and Fred and drive them to the party," your new driver announces.

What's Going on Here: Your son has had his driver's license for two weeks. Although you know he is conscientious and careful, having friends in the car is distracting and in your mind a bad idea. He needs more time behind the wheel.

Response: "We know you are responsible, but we don't feel comfortable having friends in the car yet. We'll talk about this when you have another month or two of driving under your belt."

Alert: The human brain does not fully mature until age twenty-six, so, like it or not, this is the time to give your teen facts about distractions while driving, be it friends fooling around in the car or using their cell phones while driving. Thirty-two states, including Washington, DC, do not allow novice drivers to use cell phones. Drivers are twenty-three times more likely to have an accident while texting. Driving while texting is the same as driving after drinking four beers and accounts for eleven teen deaths every day.

··· SCENARIO ···

"I don't want to talk about drugs or drinking, Dad."

What's Going on Here: Your child has reached the age at which sex, alcohol, and other drugs may tempt him. His friends, or some of them you guess, are experimenting. No matter how much pushback your child gives you, persevere in insisting on having a "talk."

Response: "I know you don't, and it's not fun for me, either. It's important for you to listen."

Alert: Don't avoid essential conversations with your adolescents because the topics are difficult. A tidbit you provide could be the one that sticks in your child's mind and makes the difference between making a foolish decision and arriving home safely. Go online together to view "teen and alcohol" underage drinking facts if you don't think your message is being absorbed or are unsure of the facts. Viewing them—including risk factors like alcohol poisoning, motor-vehicle crashes, and long-term emotional problems—is startling and powerful.

··· **SCENARIO** ···

"It's out of state, but I want to go to college with Don and Wesley," announces your soon-to-be high school graduate.

What's Going on Here: Your son has been visiting colleges with friends. Like many young people who aren't sure what they want to study, he and his buddies are attracted to the colleges reputed to be party schools. You refuse to pay out-of-state tuition unless you're convinced he'll get a solid education.

Response: "No, we're not paying for you to go on vacation for four years. Let's explore other schools. We're happy to fund your education provided you choose a reputable academic institution."

Alert: You don't have to defend your position. Be firm. Your decision is not open to debate when you bankroll the college bills.

. . . .

Parenting Is Forever: Adult Children

In spite of all its pluses, our hyper-connected society creates connections in which children have little autonomy. Parents micromanage children's lives from very young ages and in many cases raise children who can't think or act on their own, checking in with mom or dad into adulthood. When children become adults—either living with you, on their own at college, or after college in their own place—they continue to turn to you for practical, emotional, or financial support.

If you had trouble saying no when your child was younger, you may think that it's too late to break the cycle of dependence and supervision. You want to be caring, but there are circumstances in which parents' support is counter-productive, when you should be saying no to giving advice, meddling in their problems, solving their conflicts, or bailing them out financially.

You see yourself as loyal and accommodating at times to a fault. It could be time for your adult child to fend for him- or herself.

··· **SCENARIO** ···

"I'm so unhappy," your college freshman sobs into the phone. "Please let me come home."

What's Going on Here: Empty-nest syndrome can be a problem for parents as well as their children. You feel your child's pain and have been quite miserable yourself since she left. You are not opposed to her living with you and going to school locally. But you also believe she'll be stronger if she finds a way to pull through.

Response: "Take a deep breath. I know it's hard, but give it until after midterms. I'm afraid you'll regret it if you leave college this soon."

Alert: Give it time for your child to make new friends and learn her way around a school with new people and new demands. Make a later date to talk about her coming home again when you have both had more time to adapt to the separation.

⋯ SCENARIO ⋯

"I'm going to e-mail my English paper to you. Would you read it and tell me what needs to be fixed or changed?"

What's Going on Here: You "screened" your child's papers and reports from the time he started school until high school graduation. He's come to rely on your suggestions and corrections.

Response: "You're in college and on your own. I am sure you're able to edit your paper yourself."

Alert: As much as you would like to be a helpful parent, it's time for your child do his or her own work or find an editor at school. Your days as "reader" and "teacher" should have ended years ago.

⋯ SCENARIO ⋯

"Guess what, I got into that MFA program!" your daughter tells you over the phone. *"Can we chat about your cosigning a loan?"*

What's Going on Here: You are thrilled at your daughter's acceptance into a prestigious program, but surprised at her request. There were no talks of your pitching in financially, but she's assumed you'd have no objection to her putting your name on a graduate-school loan application.

Response: "We can have a chat and advise you, but don't count on our financial help. We paid for college and made it clear that anything more would be your choice."

Alert: Before signing on the dotted line, think ahead to your retirement years: will your "nest egg" be sufficient if you agree to cover her loan? There's a difference between being a big-hearted parent and making a sacrifice that will affect how you live in the future. Stress you may feel down the road could put a strain on your relationship.

⋯ SCENARIO ⋯

"Mom and Dad, we saw the most adorable house today! Will you give us money for the down payment?"

What's Going on Here: You are not shocked by this request from your adult child. After all, you've been financing her lifestyle for decades, if not wholly, then certainly a large part of it.

Response: "We really can't do that."

Alert: Be sure you are really helping—not enabling—when you come to a child's financial aid, whatever "the ask" or his or her age.

⋯ SCENARIO ⋯

"Dad, we need cat food and milk. Please get some while you're out," your adult child tells you.

What's Going on Here: Although he's living at home, he's employed and can stop at the store.

Response: "No, I think you can handle that."

Alert: Not only is it unacceptable that he tries to unload what he should be doing onto you, but it's also important to use *no* to embarrass him into acting like a grown-up.

··· SCENARIO ···

"Can you talk?" a text from your daughter reads. Less than a minute later, you get another: "I am SO ticked off. My jerk of a roommate refuses to clean." And then, another: "What do I do?" . . . "What would you do?" . . . "I am so angry."

What's Going on Here: Not your problem. Your daughter chose her roommate, and they found an apartment together. They will have to work it out themselves.

Response: "I'm pretty sure you and she can figure it out."

Alert: You remember the agony of dealing with uncooperative roommates. Jumping in to solve the issue for her may well appease your anxiety over her conflict. But if you leap in every time she's stuck, she'll never figure out how to solve differences with her peers. Consider that you may have made your child your sole focus, and it's time to ask yourself who is needier—you or your adult child?

··· SCENARIO ···

"Can you call the doctor for me and make an appointment for my checkup? I don't have the time."

What's Going on Here: Your child is in his twenties but hasn't figured out how to completely manage his own medical care.

Response: "No, you should do it."

Alert: Emphasize that your son is a capable adult no longer in need of a helicopter parent. Continuing in the same problem-solving vein has the potential to stunt an adult child's development.

··· SCENARIO ···

*"Dad, I said I would take care of it," your
daughter, who has returned to the nest after
her divorce, says in an exasperated tone. She's
warning you not to remind her again.*

What's Going on Here: Your daughter has a history of putting things off or, worse, hoping you will forget or do it for her. Her strategy of avoiding chores, even if not a conscious manipulation, is one you know all too well.

Response: "I am not happy about having to ask you over and over. You are an adult and need to share some of the household responsibilities. You are not a guest."

Alert: When an adult child, regardless of his or her age, lives with you again, there is the danger of slipping back into "mommy-daddy-ten-year-old self" habits—to the time you did most things for your child.

··· SCENARIO ···

*"Is it okay if my date spends the night?"
asks your young adult son, who has moved
back home after graduating college.*

What's Going on Here: More young adults are returning to the nest for a number of reasons, and it's natural to want to support them and not interfere in their lives as adults. But this sounds like a recipe for awkwardness to you.

Response: "That makes me very uncomfortable; we never met this young woman. I know a lot of other parents don't care, but I do. You will have to respect my feelings."

Alert: It is your house and you have every right to expect that your feelings will be honored.

··· SCENARIO ···

"You don't mind if I smoke this in front of you, right?"
your son asks, holding an unlit joint in his hand.

What's Going on Here: Your twenty-five-year-old is visiting for the holidays. You didn't allow his smoking pot as a teen, and you don't like it now.

Response: "It might not be hip of me, but it still irks me that you do this. Please choose a place outside on the patio."

Alert: Be courteous and respectful of your son's choices, but encourage him to do the same when he's in your space.

··· SCENARIO ···

"Hi, favorite mom! Can you transfer $500
into your favorite son's account?"

What's Going on Here: You roll your eyes at your son—your *only* son—and his repeated cries for financial assistance. You're trapped in a cycle: he asks for money; you lament but end up forking it over anyway. You wish you could stop but don't know how.

Response: Present evidence: "I paid your bills for the last three months. I'm not lending you more money until you pay me back. Then we can talk about another loan."

Alert: People generally don't change; you need to change your attitude and approach to the situation. Gird yourself with a *no*.

··· SCENARIO ···

Your daughter calls you at work. "Will you watch the kids a few hours this evening so I can stay at the office a little later?"

What's Going on Here: It's great that you live close to your daughter and grandchildren, but you also have a job that leaves you too exhausted to chase your rambunctious young grandchildren in the evening. You helped her out several times this week, and she probably expects you to agree again—you almost always do.

Response: "Can we talk about all the babysitting I'm doing? You know I love the kids, but . . ." Or, "I know you think watching the kids at a moment's notice is something I handle easily, but I'm having trouble keeping my energy up." Or, "I'd like some time for myself. Can we arrange a set schedule?"

Alert: As much as you don't want to turn an adult child down and as much as you love spending time with the kids, you have to take care of your life and your well-being. By keeping the lines of communication open, you'll be able to explain your limitations and/or the need for time to yourself and to keep up your own social life.

··· SCENARIO ···

"Here's the list of items I need for the garden this year. Can you pick them up so we can have everything ready for the weekend?"

What's Going on Here: Your children think that because you've retired you can readily pick up the slack for them. They think they're coming to your rescue by keeping you busy with their chores.

Response: "I know you think I have nothing to do all day, but I do. We can pick up the garden supplies first thing Saturday morning together and still have time to get everything we planned finished."

Alert: Adult children often equate "retired" with lounging around. If necessary, explain to your children you don't need them to help fill your days. Doing nothing may be exactly what you worked for all those years.

··· 5 ···

At Work

The boss and her boss sing your praises. What a good feeling. Or is it?

Whether you are the CEO, an aspiring CEO, or the most junior person on the payroll, you want to be a team player, your group to be productive, and your organization to thrive. Regardless of your position, the workplace can be a request minefield and, thus, an essential place to sharpen your *no* skills.

The consensus thinking in business is that agreeing to demands and requests, no matter how absurd, keeps bosses and clients happy. Such thinking is antiquated and can reap disastrous results. Saying no effectively not only protects your time and boundaries, but also keeps work relationships respectful and positive.

You will want to apply many of the insights and techniques for saying no to friends and family in your business life. The perks that come from incorporating the word *no* at work will help you:

- Make the best use of your time.
- Stay focused on achieving the goals you set for yourself.
- Find some of the ever-elusive work-life balance.
- Stand up for yourself while also communicating that you are supportive.

- Become better at identifying when the asker looks to you to bail him out or shoulder his responsibilities.
- Accept assignments that gain managers' respect and move you forward.
- Understand that you don't have to be aggressive or defensive when you refuse.

Unlike interacting with friends or family, sometimes you have little or no choice to refuse in the workplace. But, there's a difference between saying yes when you have to and being the person who always assumes the extra load.

Down in the office trenches, it can be hard to define your role: Are you a diligent worker, or are you the person others count on to bend over backward? What happens when you don't take time to assess how you respond to work-related requests? Use the quiz below to take a deeper look at how you operate at work.

Quiz: Are You the Office Yes-Man (or Woman)?

Which of these statements ring true for you?

1. You can't remember the last time you didn't eat lunch at your desk or work during a break or meal.
2. You regularly work more than required or than you are expected to do.
3. You often feel like there's too much on your plate but don't see a way out of any of it.
4. You fear being perceived as unreasonable or a poor team player if you turn down a task.
5. You've covered for a slacker coworker more than once.
6. You can recall at least two recent projects where you ended up contributing much more than anyone else.
7. You've agreed to requests that you aren't excited about or that aren't necessary for keeping your job.

8. You've taken on tasks that you didn't want to do to avoid displeasing a coworker.
9. You place the needs of several of the people you work with above your own. You always place your boss's needs above your own.
10. If you didn't have to see colleagues every day, you would not choose to spend time with them—yet you've been to their baby showers, to their retirement parties, and out to dinner with them more times than you can count.

A high number of *true* answers indicates it's time to start finding the right ways to say no on the job. Saying no helps maintain your focus and enhance your productivity, a key skill wherever you work.

High Performance versus Overload

Maybe you are a performance junkie who fears people will dislike you or consider you an underachiever if you don't always work in the ways asked of you. But what is it costing you?

Such high performance levels wreak havoc on your personal life—you're frequently late or forced to cancel dates. Or you spend too little time with family and friends. But most important, if you overextend yourself and become ill, you are of no help to anyone. The added stress of taking on anything and everything creates myriad negative reactions that affect your sleep, your diet, or your anxiety level—all of which can lead to errors in judgment on the job. It can also lead to a poor review—the very thing you were trying to avoid when taking on more. It's very important to you and to those you love to honor your commitments to keep stability, or some semblance of it, in your life. A life best lived is balanced.

Often bosses and colleagues in higher positions know when they are asking something beyond the normal range of what is expected. Listen for apology in their voice or tone, a slight reluctance to ask, a telltale wavering. Each is a clue that your *no* will be accepted without objection or consequence. At the very least, you'll know your superior is open to alternatives or negotiation.

Harshness bias, the worry that people will judge you unjustly, is exaggerated in most people's minds. Instead of mucking about in a quandary over whether to say *no*, spit it out. Keeping *no* handy helps you avoid unnecessary obligations that hold no possible benefit for you.

··· SCENARIO ···

You're about to step out for a much-needed lunch but hear a new message come into your inbox. "I need someone to scan this contract for errors. Please reply ASAP?" your manager writes.

What's Going on Here: Your desk is littered with to-do notes, papers from projects, and food wrappers—the by-product of eating way too many lunches at your desk. You're feeling rundown and were looking forward to some fresh air.

Response: "I need to run to lunch, I won't even be able to think straight without some food. I'll be back soon. This is at the top of my list" (if it is). Or, don't respond until you have eaten and returned to the office.

Alert: Even a thirty-minute break dedicated to your needs—and yours alone—actually helps workers charge through the rest of their day. Researchers found that these "me breaks" helped doctors at the start of their careers bounce back and work more productively, while doing the opposite leads to burnout. It's more than all right to take a break, eat, engage in physical activity, or do something unrelated to your job.

··· SCENARIO ···

*The person you work for says, "A new
client, a rush job. Can you take it on?"*

What's Going on Here: You feel the weight of another project as
soon as the question hits your ears. You can't imagine squeez-
ing in one more client, and a rush job to boot. Before answering, think about what's on your plate already and whether this
new client will move you in the direction of your goals.

Response: Assuming you want the assignment, you might say,
"Let's talk about it. I would like to handle it, but I have so
many other tasks. What can we move to someone else or put
on hold for a while?"

Alert: When you carry a full load, doing more doesn't necessarily equate to increased job security. It will, however, greatly
add to your anxiety and may reduce your effectiveness.

··· SCENARIO ···

*At four thirty the boss asks, "Can you
stay a few extra hours tonight?"*

What's Going on Here: Tough to refuse the boss, tougher still if
you've made plans. You wonder if a *no* endangers your job
security, but not showing up for your evening plans may jeop-
ardize a friendship or your love life. It's unlikely that turning
down the boss's last-minute request will put you in front of
the firing squad. A qualified *no* is in order.

Response: "I'd like to but can't tonight. I have a commitment I
can't break, but any other night this week is fine."

Alert: Weigh the situation to see if you are really needed or if your loyalty is being tested. Run a mental checklist: What work is outstanding? What are the due dates? Can you finish up during the day? Anything major upcoming that requires more than the normal preparation: a conference, a presentation, out-of-town clients visiting? Or, is this your boss's standard request because he doesn't have a life beyond the office? Is this the way he flaunts his power?

··· SCENARIO ···

"I only trust you to call these people."

What's Going on Here: What a joke. Who does your superior think she's fooling? There are other people equally qualified and experienced to make the calls.

Response: "Tim or Cynthia can handle those calls as well as I can, probably better."

Alert: Make it clear that you're onto the flattery game without saying so. Give suggestions on how the task can be accomplished to free yourself.

··· SCENARIO ···

"Can you help me finish up the Johnson project?"

What's Going on Here: You would like to help your colleague or boss, but the way the week is panning out, you'll be lucky to polish off what's urgent on your own list. Before you refuse, be sure that your *no* won't negatively affect you or your team.

Response: "I want to help you. I know the Johnson project is a huge coup for us. But it's important to me to finish what I have to do."

Alert: Saying no is very often a time-management issue; pay attention to what you have to do before accepting. Setting limits may be in order to get you out from under the *yeses* that define and bury you at—and in—work. Offer minimal assistance to a project you are turning down—to confer, advise, be a sounding board, or pitch in when you have time.

··· SCENARIO ···

"Lawrence has resigned, and I'm going to redistribute his workload between you and Allison."

What's Going on Here: You knew Lawrence planned to leave, but you didn't think his workload would be passed to you. You can't refuse, but you need additional information.

Response: "How long before we hire Lawrence's replacement?" Or, "Is this a temporary assignment?" Or, "You'll have to tell me what you want done first, since doing his work will put some of mine behind schedule."

Alert: Questions about how long you are expected to cover for a departed employee lets your boss know that additional work will be a burden. Asking for a priority agenda should lower deadline expectations and give you a bit of breathing room.

··· SCENARIO ···

*"One of my best people quit. Can you
take over for him? It's a better territory
and will mean top dollar to you."*

What's Going on Here: You've only had this job a short time, so it feels like an offer you can't refuse. You've produced and the boss wants to give you a premier position with more responsibility and more money—and considerably more time on the road, three to five days a week versus the one or two in your current position. You think anyone in his right mind would say yes. Think again. You know you can handle it but have concerns: you're in a new relationship that looks as if it could go places, which it won't if you're on the road all week every week; or perhaps you're in a new marriage, had a baby recently, or have young children you want to spend time with.

Response: "I'm really flattered that you think so highly of me, but I can't handle the additional travel right now. Thank you so much."

Alert: Analyze attractive proposals and the effect on your career *and* on your personal life so you don't wind up feeling overly burdened or putting your personal life in peril.

··· SCENARIO ···

*"Will you speak at the Colorado
conference in November?"*

What's Going on Here: Although you dislike giving presentations, November is six months away. Who plans or worries so far in advance? While you're agreeing, you'll look like a hero for filling in a vacant slot on the conference schedule.

Response: "Thank you for the opportunity, I really appreciate it, but I have to pass."

Alert: When a chore is to take place in the future, the tendency is to think about it in a generalized way, rather than about the hassles and problems involved in its execution. As the conference draws closer and preparing becomes paramount, you may begin to feel anxious and distressed with yourself for committing—a feeling hardly worth the praise you received months earlier.

··· SCENARIO ···

"I'm offering you more territory (a higher paying position, a better schedule . . .). What do you think?"

What's Going on Here: Sometimes offers sound like bonuses or promotions. It's inviting to jump at the chance. Unless you're familiar with the position, you're apt to be taken by surprise. You'd best fill in the blanks.

Response: "What a nice proposition. I can't say yes or no quite yet. I'll get back to you in a couple days."

Alert: Be sure what's being offered is really an improvement or step up in some way. Are there financial gain possibilities or career enhancement in the immediate future or down the road?

··· SCENARIO ···

Your desk phone rings.
"Is this a good time to talk?"

What's Going on Here: It's often a knee-jerk reaction to drop everything when you get a call. When you're distracted and busy, the tendency is to fall right into the conversation rather than risk offending the person on the other end of the line. You think it will only take a minute; you'll get rid of the caller right away. That usually doesn't happen. You will be much more focused on the caller and the content of the call if you arrange another time to talk.

Response: "I have to call you back. I'm in the middle of . . ." Or, "Be back to you in ten minutes; I'm finishing up something."

Alert: If the caller, even a superior, asks if you are available, she probably won't be offended if you put her off for a bit.

··· SCENARIO ···

"Let's sync up your work e-mail on your
phone," your boss suggests one day. "That
way we can always be connected."

What's Going on Here: You've noticed since starting this job that everyone is glued to their work e-mail. It's a busy company, but you cannot be expected to be at clients' beck and call twenty-four seven. Having your phone buzz or chime for each and every e-mail that comes in day, night, and on weekends would be super annoying.

Response: "I make it a point to keep a good eye on my office inbox. I'm not sure linking to my personal phone would be any better." Or, if true: "I'm fine with having a separate company phone."

Alert: Alter a request to make it acceptable and manageable. Be aware of and limit how much of your personal time you are willing to sacrifice. Emergencies or rush assignments aside, getting work-related calls at night or on weekends is an invasion of privacy and generally beyond the call of duty.

··· **SCENARIO** ···

"You're so fast!" your manager remarks as you burn through your tasks for the day. "Can you handle an additional report, by five?"

What's Going on Here: Yes, you are fast—because you want to cross things off your to-do list and go home without stressing over unfinished work. On the other hand, you believe more assignments done well means more opportunity to shine.

Response: "I'm happy you noticed. I want to do a good job on the next report, but can you push the deadline until tomorrow or the next day?"

Alert: Agreeing and failing to follow through or deliver may damage your reputation. When accepting additional duties, give yourself realistic chances for success.

··· SCENARIO ···

*A new memo comes in: "$100 gift card
to the top salesperson this month!"*

What's Going on Here: You've been pushing yourself at work, putting in long hours and working weekends. The incentive has fired up your competitive side, but the opportunity comes at a time when you have personal issues that require your attention.

Response: Tell yourself: "I'll win next time."

Alert: We often struggle with saying no to ourselves. The quest to over-perform or to outperform colleagues, to be the star, isn't always the right choice. Cut yourself some slack.

··· SCENARIO ···

*"Jolene's out sick today," your boss
announces before the weekly staff meeting.
"You can review the designs, right?"*

What's Going on Here: There's nothing on your résumé that qualifies you to do Jolene's task. You suspect you were asked because you're the youngest and the newest at the company. You immediately worry you won't do a good-enough job.

Response: "Not sure I can be as effective as Jolene, but I'm willing to try."

Alert: You can't reasonably opt out of everything. Saying no would make things awkward, but you can stress up front how your boss shouldn't expect the same analysis as someone much more experienced.

··· SCENARIO ···

"I have news for you: Your five-dollar raise request can't be granted. But, we can increase your store discount to 70 percent!"

What's Going on Here: You've worked at this clothing boutique for a couple of years and put forth what you thought was a solid argument for a raise. Your boss not only informs you that you won't get it, but tries to cushion the blow with a huge discount on merchandise. The discount is appealing—you can stock your closet for the rest of your life—but it won't help with rent or utilities.

Response: "Thanks, but to be honest I need money to pay my bills. Isn't there a middle-ground option?"

Alert: Show appreciation—even if you don't feel any—to keep the conversation open. If you end up looking for a higher-paying job and need a reference, you'll want to maintain a positive relationship with your manager.

· · · · · · · · · · · ·

Standing Up for Yourself

Occasionally taking on more than you can handle at work to move up the ladder or boost your reputation is one thing. Assuming too much responsibility and being perpetually gracious about accepting work is another. Going out of your way to do a favor for a stressed coworker or boss can turn into a problematic pattern. To whom do you think bosses and coworkers will turn when something additional has to get done? And to whom will they point when something goes awry? You, of course.

Maybe you worry your job will be in jeopardy if you say no. Or maybe it makes you happy to make someone else's job easier. Ask yourself: Am I helping a coworker more than he assists me? Do I say yes to a panicked boss's request because I want everything to run smoothly? At this point, you may have gone so far that you define yourself by your accomplishments rather than by what your job function really is.

To hone in on the tasks pertinent to your role, keep a to-do list of what you want to accomplish that day or week. With it in front of you, you'll be more inclined to refuse requests that prevent you from crossing items off the list. If a coworker pesters you for a nonessential favor, simply point and think, "Not on my list, not my priority."

··· SCENARIO ···

"I've had a really long week. Can you fill in the rest?" your coworker e-mails you. He attached his (unfinished) half of a project you were both assigned to work on equally.

What's Going on Here: No apology, no offer to have your back next time, not even a thank you. This coworker is as selfish as they come. You learned that it's better for a company if more employees are selfless—giving more to others than taking for themselves—so you're inclined to take one for the team. But then why does your coworker's request make you bristle?

Response: "Sorry you're having a bad week, but I allotted a specific amount of time to do my part. You'll have to find a way."

Alert: He's looking out for himself. The tip-off: he's acting like there's no question he deserves your favor. Devote your energy to appreciative coworkers.

··· SCENARIO ···

*"Take a second to read this for me," your
cubicle mate says, tossing a sheet of paper your
way. "I want to make sure it sounds good."*

What's Going on Here: You spend so much of any given workday reacting to other people's crises, helping out whenever needed. It's a sign of a valuable employee, right? Today's proofreading request is another little thing your coworker asks way too often. It's exhausting.

Response: "I can't right now."

Alert: A good way to tell if your benevolence is always being taken advantage of is to ask yourself, "Does this person even hesitate before asking me for a favor? Does he or she even intend to return the favor?" Only say yes to favors that you know you can do and still feel energized. If you don't feel happy when being generous, you risk turning into an employee who doesn't want to help anyone, ever.

··· SCENARIO ···

*"I'm coming with you to the meeting. I'll be
there to back you up and give support."*

What's Going on Here: Colleagues who are excessively involved in your career can be intrusive to a point where you feel stifled. They stick with you every step of the way because they think they are shielding you or because they believe associating with you makes them look important.

Response: "It's so nice of you to offer, but I have to tackle this one myself."

Alert: Decide if this person is being truly supportive or if he is latching on to your favorable position in the company or to what he construes as your current or future success.

··· SCENARIO ···

"That's not a flattering photo on your LinkedIn profile," your office mate tells you. "You should really choose a more professional one."

What's Going on Here: Your coworker, always the dictatorial one, likes telling you what to do. Because he's been at the company longer than you have, you tend to believe he knows what he's talking about but are tired of his uninvited critiques.

Response: "Thanks for your suggestion." Or, "I will take your suggestion under advisement."

Alert: The best career advice is usually positive and comes from people who have your best interests at heart.

··· SCENARIO ···

The boss requests the year-end analysis. "Can you have it to me by Friday?"

What's Going on Here: You've known the due date for months but haven't worked on it because of other, more pressing assignments. The boss knows you're not a slacker; if you could work up what he needs by Friday, you would. If you promise the year-end analysis for Friday, you'll be up all night. It's wiser to be straightforward and see what the boss wants you to do.

Response: "No, I can't have it ready. I need an extension."

Alert: Making promises you can't fulfill makes you look incompetent. Keep your boss informed when new projects interfere with or slow down others. Negotiate a new due date.

··· SCENARIO ···

"I know you don't want to do this, but would you write up your notes from yesterday's session?"

What's Going on Here: The significant words are not what you are being asked to do, but *how* you are being asked. You think, he's reluctant to ask—he's coming at this from a nice place. The preface "I know you don't want to do this" aims to cleverly break down your resistance.

Response: "I'm backed up; I don't know when I can get to that."

Alert: Listen for statements that chisel away at your resistance and are designed to make you more willing.

··· SCENARIO ···

"This mailing is huge and has to go out by the end of the day. Will you stuff envelopes during lunch?"

What's Going on Here: A reputation for reliability is usually a plus, but not when peers turn to you regularly for tedious jobs. To break the cycle, start refusing chores that earn you nothing more than a pat on the back. Keep it simple.

Response: "Wish I could help, but I can't today."

Alert: Agree sometimes, but not all the time. As soon as coworkers pick up on the fact that you're no longer willing to do the grunt work as a matter of course, they'll hesitate before asking. Bosses are a different story; tread lightly with the nos when they ask for the small stuff.

··· SCENARIO ···

*"I need you to come walk my dog at
7:00 p.m.," your boss texts you, her assistant,
at 6:45. "I have a dinner meeting."*

What's Going on Here: You rely on the extra dog-walking money and have learned to deal with your boss's narcissistic tendencies, but this last-minute request crosses a line. Your commuter train is approaching your stop. No way do you want to turn around and head back toward the office and her home.

Response: Appeal to logic. "I'm on the train and two seconds from my stop. I can't make it back in time for his walk. Let me know when I should plan to stay later and I will gladly walk him whenever with advance notice."

Alert: It's not easy to keep a smooth relationship with a demanding boss. If you want to keep your job, avoid a direct, harsh *no*. It's better to stay calm and appeal to reason than to start a fight that in the long run you will lose anyway.

··· SCENARIO ···

*You receive a LinkedIn invitation in your
inbox. "Hope all is well at your new job!"
a former coworker messages along with a
friend request. "I'd love to connect and buy
you a coffee to discuss how it's going."*

What's Going on Here: You heard that since you changed jobs, he's
been let go and likely wants an in at your new company. You
clashed with this coworker in the past and find his ladder-
climbing tactics a bit slimy.

Response: "My schedule is so packed. Let's touch base in a couple of months."

Alert: Take care about burning professional bridges that you
may need at some point. If you run into each other in person,
chalk up not getting together to your being busy.

··· SCENARIO ···

*"Do me a favor and go over Jerome's
report and let me know what you think.
It's an imposition, I know, but . . ."*

What's Going on Here: Note the asker's hesitation and wavering.
Jerome doesn't work in your department, and you're not
entirely sure what his report is about. The person asking may
be trying to protect himself by getting another opinion. You
also don't want to encroach on someone else's territory. Provide a rationale when you can.

Response: "No, I don't know enough about this project to give a sound review. Someone in Jerome's department could provide more valuable insights."

Alert: Masquerading as a know-it-all backfires. Saying "I don't know enough" is acceptable even when the asker believes otherwise. Don't offer feeble excuses that sound like "The dog ate my homework." You gain more points for honesty. Whenever possible, suggest or negotiate a solution that takes you out of the picture but still gets the job accomplished.

··· SCENARIO ···

"A new assistant starts in the morning.
I'd like you to train her."

What's Going on Here: The whole staff knew you back when you were the "newbie" at the desk outside a manager's office. They still see you in that job sometimes. You've worked your way up to the impressive position you now hold.

Response: "I'd be happy to, but I have a presentation tomorrow (an appointment, a big job to finish). I can't take the time. Don't you think she'd feel more comfortable learning from another assistant?"

Alert: Once pegged the trainer, you will have to remind people subtly that that's not your role anymore.

··· SCENARIO ···

"You're young and savvy, can you teach the marketing department how to use Twitter?" your manager asks.

What's Going on Here: You're relatively new to this office, and everyone sees you as the young, tech-savvy dream hire who can double as the IT Department (with no extra pay, of course). You've already offered some tech advice but are by no means a social media guru. Your boss hopes to avoid dealing with the issue by transferring the problem to you.

Response: "Thanks for asking me, but my skills and knowledge aren't as strong as you think. You may want to hire a full-time social media marketer or consider hiring an outside consultant for a short period."

Alert: Acknowledge the bind or problem your refusal may cause. Offering a solution makes a *no* more acceptable. Convey clarity in your reasoning in the most straightforward manner so the person you turn down recognizes that you want to be helpful.

··· SCENARIO ···

"Aidan, can you show me how to transfer those files again?" an older coworker calls from across the office.

What's Going on Here: You have shown this Luddite how to do basic functions on his desktop several times now without complaint. But then again, he showed you the ropes in your first few months on the job.

Response: "Sure. Let me also write down instructions for you to make things extra clear."

Alert: Leaning on you as a tech instructor isn't a good use of your time. Step-by-step notes emphasize that these are things he can do himself.

··· SCENARIO ···

"When you go to lunch, would you pick up a bottle of aspirin and a pair of black pantyhose for me?"

What's Going on Here: You are an assistant, not a personal assistant. The bottom of the office totem pole can feel like a harrowing place, but that's where it's important to learn how to stand up for yourself.

Response: "I brought my lunch today and am not going out of the building." Or, "I'm meeting someone for lunch and won't have time." Or, "If I do that, I won't be able to finish the work you've given me."

Alert: Start being your boss's personal shopper and errand runner and the next thing you know you'll spend lunch hours buying kitty litter for her cat and get-well cards for her sick relatives.

··· SCENARIO ···

"I have a feeling that others on the team aren't happy with the new system—but you're on board with me, right?"

What's Going on Here: Your boss is on a rather unpopular mission to change the way the team stays organized, and other staffers see it as unfair micromanaging. Your boss expects you to validate his idea. You don't think it's a good one and have expressed this to your coworkers. You've told white lies to him in the past in order to look like more of a dedicated employee, but you fear your coworkers are getting annoyed at your kissing up.

Response: "I understand your vision, but I'm not sure it's clicking with everyone. I think we need to tweak your concept."

Alert: Agreeing with your boss may put you in his good graces in the short run but dig you into a problematic hole with teammates or those who work under you. Support those you work closely with by stating your reservations.

· · · · · · · · · · ·

When You're the Boss

For the yes-prone, being a boss at any level is a daily seesaw. You want to maintain positive rapport with those who work for you and with your clients or customers. That can mean joking, bonding over television shows, or meeting spouses and families. Boundaries so easily blur.

Even the most skilled in upper-level positions face issues calling for a *no*. Being in a position of authority brings complicated requests, opportunities for tension, and multilevel obligations. Tasked with employee workloads and different personalities, office relationships and watching the bottom line for the company and clients, bosses see power dynamics get messy.

For people-pleasing leaders, falling into a yes-habit can result in strife that affects staff harmony, client relationships, and productivity. Sometimes, stressed bosses grant an employee request without thoroughly considering it, merely to make it go away. Agreeing to requests—specifically, those that realistically cannot or should not be accommodated— can hinder your ability to lead effectively.

Heavy doses of acquiescing can lead to brusque, sometimes volatile reactions. It's generally better for a boss to keep a consistent hard line with employees rather than be kind-hearted one moment and boorish the next. Those who receive more predictable, consistent treatment from a superior likely experience less stress than those who aren't sure how the boss will react.

Simply put, if you are in charge, it's healthier for everyone to keep the word *no* close at hand. Use language that turns people down but still tells those who work for you that you value them. Be clear and transparent in terms of how your *no* relates to the assignment, company, or client.

··· SCENARIO ···

"I'll have the presentation finished by noon on Saturday. I will e-mail it to you, so watch your phone," one of your hardworking employees tells you on Friday morning.

What's Going on Here: Your employees have become slaves to both their work and their personal cell phones, and it's not helping anyone's performance.

Response: "That's not necessary. I don't keep my phone on during weekends, and neither should you. We all need a break. I'll look at it first thing Monday."

Alert: Recent surveys show that being constantly plugged in can have negative effects on work relationships and employee well-being. The pressure to be connected to work during nights and weekends can cause poor performance and anxiety. More workplaces are encouraging their employees to unplug.

··· SCENARIO ···

*"I really need this job. Can you
hire me on a trial basis?"*

What's Going on Here: You desperately need help, and she has a great résumé and seems to be a decent person. However, you sense a bit of aggressiveness that might work in another department, but not yours. The applicant's forwardness is going to grate on the people she'll be working with.

Response: "You're not right for our needs at the moment."

Alert: Always go with your first reaction—particularly when you know the other personalities involved—even if it means everyone will have to work a bit harder until you fill the vacant slot.

··· SCENARIO ···

*"Brian's organizing system is nuts. I'm afraid he'll
lose track of something important. Can you tell him?"*

What's Going on Here: A fastidious employee takes issue with his cubicle mate's messiness and asks you to play referee. The request is a waste of your time, and you don't want employees to look at you as someone they can tattle to. Then again, you sympathize with his annoyance.

Response: "Have you mentioned this to Brian? I'm thinking you could help him get organized without my being the heavy. Try that first."

Alert: Stepping in like a parent puts an unnecessary burden on you.

··· SCENARIO ···

*"I'm so, so, so sorry for not sending that news
blast on time," a member of the tech group
apologizes. "This doesn't compromise my chance
at that promotion we talked about, does it?"*

What's Going on Here: Your employee, while bright and usually very responsible, made a huge mistake that put you in hot water with a few important clients as well as your superiors. After the smoke cleared, it led you to question his ability to take on more responsibility. He is remorseful, and you don't like the idea of telling him that now he might not get a promotion.

Response: "You are usually on point, but this error didn't come at the best time. I'll see what I can do to get the others to overlook it."

Alert: Don't promise it will be okay. Explain that you alone do not make promotion decisions. Emphasize that you appreciate his dedication and will do the best you can for him.

··· SCENARIO ···

*A text arrives before you reach the office.
"Hey boss, I have to bring Lindsay to the
hospital again. Not able to come in today."*

What's Going on Here: Your employee is in a difficult bind. You want to be cognizant of family pressures and emergencies; you've granted extra personal days with no questions asked because her work is top-notch. The staff covers for her as best they can, and you see they are disgruntled.

Response: "Sorry to hear that. Next time you're in, let's discuss how we can help you tend to your daughter's needs in a way so you don't fall behind."

Alert: Being a boss requires being understanding even in the toughest of circumstances. Show your support and empathy, but also let her be part of figuring out what works for everyone affected by her absences.

··· SCENARIO ···

"The client is being ridiculous," your strongest employee says in frustration. "How am I supposed to work with these unrealistic demands? Can this project be transferred to someone else?"

What's Going on Here: Your employee has valid reasons to be upset, but he is the right person and the only one in the office who can deal with the client. Switching the account to another person sends the wrong message to the client.

Response: "No argument. The client is frustrating, but I believe you are the best match for them. Let's figure out how you can better react every time they put up what feels like a roadblock."

Alert: It's not only about making sure your employees fulfill demands; it's about mentoring them toward solutions. Take care to not badmouth the client yourself, which can de-motivate your employee.

••• SCENARIO •••

"This is bull!" one of your employees screams, loud enough for those nearby to hear. "Peter comes into work late over and over again, and I'm the one who has to do his job until he arrives. You can't keep letting him sail through. He needs to go."

What's Going on Here: You hate when this employee—who is a hard worker but hot-tempered—gets worked up and puts you on the spot in front of the staff. In the past, you've tried to get these blowups over with as soon as possible by sweeping issues under the rug or bending to his requests. He has a point about Peter slacking off, but his public outbursts set a dangerous precedent, making it seem like anyone with a vendetta against another employee can yell at you.

Response: "Calm down. You have a legitimate complaint, and we will explore it together with Peter in the meeting."

Alert: The only way around out-of-control emotion is steady, composed leadership, which your livid employee will hopefully copy.

••• SCENARIO •••

"I'm not seeing results from the marketing campaign," a new client e-mails you. "I'm afraid I'm seeing money go nowhere. Can you reduce your rates?"

What's Going on Here: You expressed to this new client at the start of the process that it takes time to build traction, but patience doesn't seem to be her strong suit. You don't want to undermine yourself, but you do want to keep the client happy.

Response: "I hear you, but I assure you it takes a bit more time before you see concrete results. I can't bring down my rates, but we can talk about reducing hours. Although in my experience, more time spent on the campaign is really what makes the magic happen."

Alert: Try to amicably strike a compromise without devaluing your work.

··· SCENARIO ···

"Can I drop by your office tomorrow afternoon to ask you a few questions?" a new recruit e-mails you.

What's Going on Here: Tomorrow afternoon is actually the worst time, as it's rife with meetings and phone calls.

Response: "That won't work. How about the next day? I have time at eleven, two, and four."

Alert: Responding with a short "I'll be too busy" or "No, sorry" signals that the employee is insignificant. Without offering specific availability, you send a message that he might interpret as "I'm simply an underling" or "Whatever I want is unimportant."

··· SCENARIO ···

"I'm embarrassed to ask, but I need an advance on next month's paycheck. Possible?"

What's Going on Here: You know that your employee is going through a rough patch. He's recently had a baby (his child had an expensive surgery, he's bought a house, his wife lost her job), and you understand the financial strain he's under.

Response: "What you're asking goes against company policy. I'm sorry."

Alert: You would be seriously questioned if you authorized what amounts to a cash advance for one of your people. Option: help him out from your personal account to avoid compromising your standing at work.

··· SCENARIO ···

A client calls, yelling into the phone. "Things changed on our end. Overnight everything to me so I have it in the morning. No excuses, I mean it, or you're fired."

What's Going on Here: The difficult client—he's been that way since day one. He drives you and your staff to the limits. At some point you have to ask yourself if the money is worth the aggravation. Wouldn't the office be better off if you expended your energy finding a more pleasant and reasonable client?

Response: "It won't be ready. We were told we had until the end of the week, and we'll be ready then."

Alert: Threats and intimidation create incredible strain. Do you need such an inflexible client? Before you dump the client, evaluate the financial loss, decide how to replace him, and make sure that everyone who should be involved in the decision is consulted.

··· SCENARIO ···

"Hey boss, you want to come with us to happy hour?"

What's Going on Here: You were once in the trenches with these coworkers, and since being promoted you are thrilled that they still like you enough to want to hang out. Will continuing the closeness you once shared undermine your new authority? If you refuse, will they find you less likable?

Response: "I can't tonight, guys. I have early dinner plans."

Alert: It's a manager's job—some see it as a problem—to draw that line between business and pleasure. If asked again, go to test the waters to find out if hanging out compromises your boss-employee relationship.

. . . .

Mixing Business with Pleasure

Whether you're the boss, greenhorn, or someone in between, interacting with colleagues outside the office presents trials. Social media, where decorum dictates it's only polite to accept a workmate's friend request, has made it harder to clearly define boundaries between true friends and coworkers.

If you're like most people, there's a fine line between those at work in your friend category and those you would rather not spend off-duty hours with if you don't have to. Unless the decision affects your standing in some way, you will be more inclined to spend out-of-office time with those who have the dual standing as coworker *and* friend.

What seems on the surface like a pleasant invitation could feel like a major intrusion to you. If, for example, you're friendly with a coworker, attending her wedding will be delightful. If the coworker is merely another person in the office to you, the wedding will be an expensive annoyance, absorbing a chunk of a weekend. When you are clear about the people at work whom you consider personal friends versus those you view primarily as business associates, deciding whether to mix your business and social life becomes less complicated.

Predetermining your business inner circle as well as your position on moral issues revolving around business accomplishes two goals: you know what you want and what you are willing to do and with whom, and you're less likely to be pulled into situations in which you chastise yourself for not having considered the inconvenience or possible repercussions.

··· SCENARIO ···

*"We should carpool to work. I go
practically right past your house."*

What's Going on Here: Sharing the commute has its advantages— company when you're stuck in traffic, time to rehash the day's events or to discuss work-related problems, and paying less for gas. Yet you know yourself: You'll be nervous if he's a few minutes late to pick you up, if you want to leave early for a date or commitment to the kids, or if you want to work later than your travel buddy. You won't be able to make spur-of-the-moment decisions to go out after work or come in a bit later if you've been out on the town the night before. You may prefer to listen to an audio book or a news program rather than talk about the office.

Response: "It's a good idea, but my hours are erratic." Or, "I use the time to unwind and listen to music. Thanks for asking."

Alert: If you think your flexibility will be curtailed or his or your last-minute schedule changes will be frustrating, drive yourself.

··· SCENARIO ···

"Lunch at 1:00?" your coworker messages you from her cubicle. "I'll meet you at our table."

What's Going on Here: For no particular reason, you're having one of those days where you need to eat by yourself, perhaps peruse social media or answer texts from your mom. The last time you tried to take time for yourself, you told this coworker you needed to catch up on work, but she caught you Snap-chatting, and you don't want to feel like having to explain yourself again.

Response: "I'm having an off day. Please don't take offense, but I need to relax solo for about an hour."

Alert: Everyone needs some space. Emphasize that to your coworker.

··· SCENARIO ···

You get several e-mail notices at once: Sierra, your new office mate as of Monday, wants to be friends with you on LinkedIn, Facebook, Snapchat, Instagram, and Twitter. "Hey girl!" she writes in the message, with a friendly emoji.

What's Going on Here: Your new coworker is sweet and you get along . . . so far. You roll your eyes that she wants to be friends in every way possible before you've even had your first department meeting. You've bonded too soon with people in the past, and when trying to pull back, they acted offended.

Response: Let the requests remain pending. If she asks in person, say, "I'm slow on social media, but I'll get to your requests as soon as I can."

Alert: It's reasonable to remain suspect of a new employee until you've figured out how you want to categorize the relationship.

••• **SCENARIO** •••

"You work out at the gym up the street after work, don't you? Being your gym buddy would motivate me to exercise and, boy, could I use the motivation."

What's Going on Here: You relish your forty-five-minute spin class and don't need any incentive to get you there. You like going alone; it gives you a chance to think about something other than work.

Response: "It's the only time I have to myself all day. It's nothing personal. I hope you understand."

Alert: Be protective of the little private time you have if you don't need or want company while you exercise.

··· SCENARIO ···

You're pouring yourself a cup of eggnog at the annual holiday office party and your boss approaches you: "I've been thinking about our presentation for next week. What do you think if we change the focus?"

What's Going on Here: The entire office is relaxing, but your boss can't get his mind off work. Part of the reason why you're in your boss's good graces is because he can always come to you with ideas, but he's essentially turning a fun gathering into another meeting.

Response: "I would so prefer to talk about this on Monday when I'm fresh and ready to go. What are your children up to these days?"

Alert: It can feel odd telling your boss that you don't want to engage in shoptalk. Change the subject; someone's children are generally a safe bet.

··· SCENARIO ···

You're at your desk, and your phone chimes with a new text on a group thread between you and two other coworkers. "He's being the WORST today, right?" a coworker texts about your boss.

What's Going on Here: You occasionally text your coworkers and you are on friendly terms, but you wince at gossiping in such a public, traceable way. What if your boss sees the messages somehow? What if others notice you're "talking" on your phones and not including them?

Response: "Let's chat about it later."

Alert: Office gossip is dangerous on so many levels. Protect yourself by insisting that venting about the boss be done in a discrete, private way.

··· SCENARIO ···

"I have to get this off my chest: Amber is such an idiot. I gave her explicit instructions and she screwed up yet again," an agitated coworker tells you in the break room.

What's Going on Here: Your coworker rightly does not want to blow up at Amber but thinks he can let off steam by complaining to and seeking advice from you.

Response: "I prefer to not get involved. I'm guessing HR can give you some ideas on how to handle the problem."

Alert: Don't be flattered by his coming to you, even if it's a sign he may value your insight or allegiance. Allowing him to get things off his chest has the potential to sour your opinion of the coworker, whom you may find yourself working closely with one day. Make it your policy to stay away from office drama.

··· SCENARIO ···

"See you at the office party?"

What's Going on Here: Most office parties are not command appearances, although we often think they are. If you're married with children or have other social obligations, bosses and colleagues will understand you can't be there. Most companies evaluate performance during business hours, not on how well you socialize or move on the dance floor.

Response: "I won't be able to make it this year."

Alert: Two days after the party, few, if anyone, will remember whether or not you attended.

··· SCENARIO ···

"We're having a baby shower for Ellen the last Saturday of this month. You'll be there, yes?"

What's Going on Here: Between work-related weddings, birthdays, dinners, Friday-night beers, and weekend parties, you could virtually wipe personal friends out of your life. If you say yes to one office-related invitation, are you obligated to the others? How do you draw the line without offending someone?

Response: "I can't be there, but I will chip in on the gift."

Alert: Figure out which people are key to your position and which people you classify as friends to help you decide the must-attend festivities.

··· SCENARIO ···

You get a Facebook notification: "You're invited to join the group '3rd floor accounting team'!"

What's Going on Here: You don't mind being Facebook friends with a few select coworkers, but the larger group will surely lead to friend requests from those you don't necessarily want to interact with outside the office.

Response: Don't join; talk to a trusted coworker in person instead: "I don't go on Facebook that much. If there are any coworker events mentioned on the group that I should know about, would you shoot me an e-mail?"

Alert: Joining office Facebook groups is rarely a job requirement.

··· SCENARIO ···

"You haven't been to the restaurant strip downtown? It's killer, there are so many options," a cute coworker at your new company says. "Here, give me your number and I'll text you about it."

What's Going on Here: You obviously caught the eye of your new coworker. The request for your cell number straddles the personal-professional line. You don't want to encourage a deeper connection, but you don't want to come off as cold.

Response: "It's better to e-mail me at the office address. You already have it."

Alert: To avoid risking an uncomfortable work situation, maintain distance up front. You can backtrack later if you decide you want to pursue something more.

··· SCENARIO ···

Olivia drops two resort brochures on your desk and says, "Come with me. We'll have such a good time."

What's Going on Here: You're friendly with Olivia, but not *that* friendly. Sharing a room, lazing on a beach, and three meals a day is more bonding time than you want with anyone in your office. Nine to five Monday through Friday and occasional drinks after work are enough togetherness.

Response: "These places look fabulous, but I'm set for vacation this year." Or, "I usually go on holiday with old friends." Or, "I prefer to go away by myself." Or, "I'm using my vacation for family obligations." Or, "Those places are more money than I want to spend." Or, "I'm staying home this year to save for Cancún." (Go with the truth.)

Alert: If the thought of a coworker getting too close bothers you, don't entertain the idea of vacationing together. Away from the office you may be inclined to share more details of your life than you want known in the office.

. . . .

Sticky Situations

In the world of work—and out of it—nervy people ask just about anything of anybody. Anyone who has ever had a job has experienced that person at work who manages to always make things difficult. These people, assertive and guaranteed to be the ones to throw a wild request your way, can be your boss, your coworker, or even a pushy client.

Many of the problems encountered in the work environment come from the people in charge, the people you work for, who may laud their position and the power it gives them. For some of them, work is their life; their very being is synonymous with the office or job. When a person's world revolves around work and being successful, his or her demands can be unreasonable.

Difficult workmates continually overstep your boundaries and think nothing of it. Getting others to do something for them or using their power to get what they want is how "users" operate. You can change that. Negotiate alternatives by being clear about what you want. Avoid weakening a *no* with words that project uncertainty—*just* or *sorry*. They indicate doubt in your answer and may validate the asker's idea that the request is within his or her rights.

Below are some examples to guide you through more awkward and complicated situations.

··· SCENARIO ···

*"I need to leave early. Will you tell the boss
I wasn't feeling well if you're asked?"*

What's Going on Here: Your colleague never looked healthier. He's asking you to lie for him and probably wouldn't do the same for you. Most important, he won't like you any better or any less if you refuse.

Response: "I don't feel good about doing that. Why don't you leave the boss a note?"

Alert: Don't compromise your principles to bail out someone else.

··· SCENARIO ···

*"Will you drop this package off at Gordon's for me?
He wants to go over these reports tonight. It's on
your way," your good friend at the office asks.*

What's Going on Here: Not on the way exactly. To go to Gordon's you have to take a different, more trafficked route home, and there's often nowhere to park in his neighborhood. Then, if Gordon isn't there, he'll come to your house to pick it up. Either way, he'll involve you in a lengthy conversation. (It's impossible to cut Gordon short, he's a talker.)

Response: "Not going to work; I'm meeting friends and will be home late" (if true). Or, "I'm going in the other direction tonight" (if true). Or a simple, "I cannot do that tonight."

Alert: Bad idea to measure your self-worth in terms of what you do for others. You probably have done or will do many errands for this friend.

··· SCENARIO ···

"Please call this client back for me. He's not easy. Since he doesn't know you as well, maybe he'll take the information without his usual hundred questions."

What's Going on Here: You have your own impossible clients, but you don't look around the office for a stool pigeon to make calls for you, and neither should your coworker. Without telling him so, give him options that don't involve you.

Response: "Why don't you send him an e-mail? Or send a fax? It will seem awfully odd if I call."

Alert: Offering plausible alternatives voices your refusal and keeps you out of no-win situations without having to say, "Are you kidding? What makes you think I'm going to do the unpleasant part of your job for you?"

··· SCENARIO ···

"How about we work on this project together?"

What's Going on Here: When confronted by a coworker you know is irresponsible, doesn't carry his own weight in joint efforts, or whose work ethic drives you crazy, protect yourself when you answer.

Response: "No, I told Amy I'd work with her." Or, "I'm probably going to work with Tyrone." Or, "I can't take on anything else right now."

Alert: You don't ever have to provide lengthy excuses, and you certainly don't want to say anything hurtful to the other person when you decline.

··· SCENARIO ···

"Can you cover the Toronto meeting for me? I'll owe you one."

What's Going on Here: As with personal friends, there are colleagues who make across-the-board, vacant promises. Be sure this one's for real by asking:

Response: "I'll take you up on the offer. Can you handle the Atlanta meeting for me?"

Alert: Test people's word beforehand, not after. If you can't be assured of quid pro quo, *no* should slide right out of your mouth.

··· SCENARIO ···

"I have sent you several e-mails on the Longstreet project. I need your written reply right away." The messages arrive from the head of a branch office who is technically your boss even though you work several states apart.

What's Going on Here: This isn't the first time the boss has bombarded you with e-mails and wants written responses. You don't want what you have to say documented in e-mails, and you don't want to agitate the boss by ignoring him.

Response: In a brief e-mail, you might say, "Please, call me when you have a few minutes to discuss the Longstreet project."

Alert: When correspondence involves sensitive material or information you don't want documented, have a conversation about how you would like to communicate going forward. Let the person know that you feel more comfortable having voice contact or that direct contact sparks ideas and solutions for you.

··· SCENARIO ···

"You have to bring in more contracts (clients, business, jobs). I don't care how you get them."

What's Going on Here: Without actually saying so, the person you work for is telling you to employ any method possible, aboveboard or not. He's out-and-out bullying you into using tactics you don't agree with or know to be unethical.

Response: "We need to talk about this; I have a problem with some of what you're suggesting."

Alert: When asked to do something unethical, address it head-on. Making your position clear tells the boss that he can't bully you or ask you to compromise your principles. You've announced the line you will not cross.

··· SCENARIO ···

"Do you like the new company logo/design?"

What's Going on Here: You dislike it intensely and think it's all wrong for its intended purpose, but you are fearful of wounding its creator's ego and/or never being asked for your opinion again.

Response: "I have some reservations" is an off-putting *no*, but a *no* that gets your point across.

Alert: If you're going to have to work with or live with the design (or a business decision that impacts you) for a long time, you need to express your thoughts and offer constructive criticism.

··· SCENARIO ···

"I'm adding my name to the finished report, if it's okay with you."

What's Going on Here: Sure, she helped pull the loose ends together, checked the punctuation, and ran off the copies. She offered useful content, but one out of fifty ideas doesn't merit a full credit line. She's being bold and stretching the importance of her contribution.

Response: Smile warmly and say, "Not on this one. I worked too long and too hard. Perhaps next time."

Alert: If your hard work is the major mark of the report, don't allow others who don't deserve recognition to dilute your effort or praise, if there's any coming.

··· SCENARIO ···

"You can't leave us," the members of your professional organization (investment or other work-related group) beg you. "Please stay?"

What's Going on Here: You've been a member for many years, but you've been wrestling with the amount of preparation time stolen out of your workweek and the valuable information and advice you give versus what you get in return. Bottom line, the two are not equal.

Response: "I can't do this anymore. I'll miss you all and our meetings."

Alert: All you have is your time. Once you get those hours back, you won't feel like a deserter for very long.

··· SCENARIO ···

"You have to tell me whether to take this job."

What's Going on Here: This person wants you to take responsibility for his choices. If he accepts the job and is content, he'll believe he made the decision himself. If he loathes the job, it will be your fault and you'll hear about it, possibly for a long time.

Response: "No, it has to be your decision."

Alert: Don't go there. In general you don't get credit for the good decisions you help people make, only responsibility for the ones that turn out poorly.

••• **SCENARIO** •••

> *Your boss issues a memo: "Full-time employees are not permitted to take on additional work outside of the company."*

What's Going on Here: You understand your boss wants employees to stay focused, but you don't get paid enough to give up your weekend restaurant shift (freelance work, part-time nanny job, consulting).

Response: "Does this mean raises are in store? I'm not sure I can afford to turn away other paying gigs when I have bills every month. As long as I do them on nights and weekends and it doesn't interfere with my work, I don't see the issue."

Alert: As long as you're not working for direct competitors or on the company's time, there shouldn't be confusion or conflicts. See if you can convince your employer that your side job is a necessity.

••• **SCENARIO** •••

> *"Please e-mail me the numbers from the Freeman file I was working on before I started my new job."*

What's Going on Here: You work with sensitive, confidential data. You know you are not supposed to divulge any details, and certainly not the type of information your former colleague wants.

Response: "If I send what you want, I could lose my job. I'm sure you understand how risky that is."

Alert: Protect your position within the company. A breach of confidentiality is unlikely to be worth the "maybe" payback.

··· SCENARIO ···

You get a call on your office phone from a number you don't recognize. "I'm wondering if you're happy at your new job," the caller, a manager from a rival company, says. "Can you talk?"

What's Going on Here: No, you can't talk—you're at work, and people will easily hear what you say. You're annoyed by this person's lack of discretion but are curious to know what he wants.

Response: "I can't talk right now. Is there a number to call you back later in the day or early this evening?"

Alert: It makes sense to know what opportunities are available in your field, but protect your current job by communicating on your own terms.

··· SCENARIO ···

*"I hope you can go to the conference out of town
next week. Ellie has two young children and it's
impossible for her to be away for three days."*

What's Going on Here: You cover for Ellie when meetings run late, when work requires travel, or when a project demands over-time. Ellie, on the other hand, gets a pass; she leaves meet-ings or works from home because she is a mother and you are not. After almost a year of being Ellie's reliable backup, the arrangement is starting to feel lopsided.

Response: "Of course I'll fly out and cover the conference next week, but it is difficult for me to cover every out-of-town event" (assuming you weren't hired to do so). "Is there a way we can figure out who else can supervise some of the 'away' meetings?"

Alert: Your *yes* response is a short-term commitment but lim-its your ability to cover for Ellie (or anyone else) on a regu-lar basis. Although it may appear to your employer that you don't have a life because you don't have children, you probably do. You want your own boundaries respected, if only to have time to pursue interests or relax. It is more than reasonable to address the "Ellie" issue.

··· SCENARIO ···

*"I'm inclined to take you off the new project,"
the head of the department informs you.
"Arlene brought up a good point: your baby
is due in three months, and that's about
when the bulk of the work will happen."*

What's Going on Here: Arlene has been gunning for your job since you joined the organization. Going behind your back is infuriating; using your pregnancy as a scapegoat is grounds for a complaint to HR. The fact that your boss may have caved without consulting you is even more perplexing.

Response: "No, I'm passionate about and qualified for this project, and I'd like a fair chance to argue the case on why I am pretty sure I can do it."

Alert: Your boss might not have realized Arlene was coming from a place of sabotage. Good to know: the employee who comes off as more rational and levelheaded has the best chance of coming out on top.

··· SCENARIO ···

*"I found the perfect job for me at the same place
your friend Stella works. I'm applying for it.
Will you be one of my references or call Stella
and ask her to put in a good word for me?"*

What's Going on Here: You're in a precarious position because you don't classify this person's work as superior. She's not a close friend, and you'd rather not go out on a limb for her. If you call Stella, you're putting your reputation on the line. If she doesn't work out, Stella will never trust your recommendations again.

Response: A noncommittal answer is called for. "I don't think Stella's in a position to help very much." Or, "Let me think how I can approach Stella." Or, the self-protective standby, "I'm not going to be very influential. You should be able to get a stronger reference than me."

Alert: Within any given field, the business world is small. Recommending people you don't have faith in could reflect negatively on your ability to judge people—something that could come back to haunt you should you embark on a job hunt of your own.

··· **SCENARIO** ···

"You have to change your vacation. We need you at the year-end planning session."

What's Going on Here: You would like to attend this very important company event, but your vacation was blocked on the office calendar eight months ago—long before the session dates were posted. Your trip has been confirmed and your expenses paid. You're important but not essential, and yet you feel as if you might miss something. Canceling your vacation at this point is unreasonable, and the people you work for should understand.

Response: "I'm very torn, but I can't be there. I'll be sure someone is up-to-date and fully informed in my area to cover for me." Or, "I will give you my thoughts before I leave for vacation."

Alert: If you give in to the pressure and loyalty you feel, work will always take precedent over your personal time.

··· SCENARIO ···

"Can you stop in and show me exactly what to do again? I'm swamped since you retired and can't remember everything you told me."

What's Going on Here: You're new to the blissful life of retirement, much to the chagrin of your former work associates who continue to rely on you. Your mentee is scrambling in the wake of your absence, but you're not ready to go back to the office to give onsite instruction.

Response: "I can't today. E-mail me a list of vital items you need help with. You're probably doing better than you think."

Alert: As much as you empathize with your former colleague's panic, he and the office will adjust without you needing to drop everything and rush in. Kick back and enjoy your hike, exercise class, or eighteen holes.

··· 6 ···

Really Difficult People

Saying no is daunting no matter who is asking, demanding, or badgering you. What's disconcerting is that in many instances you can be more successful saying no to your boss or a meddlesome parent than to a stranger—the person you hired to build a deck or color your hair or met recently in the park, for instance. People you hardly know or don't know at all.

Those whose job or mission it is to sell their wares, close deals, sign you up for a subscription, or proselytize their personal viewpoints come across as sure of themselves. They project themselves to be so right or self-righteous that you become defenseless. Their tenacity wears you down. Forceful people make refusing feel as if you are trying to scale an icy cliff without the proper gear, slipping back with each step you take.

When the belief that someone knows more than you do combines with the slightest personal insecurity, intimidation clouds your ability to be decisive and firm. The woman who owns the Wool Shop may crochet better than you do, but that doesn't mean she can dictate the color or style afghan that will look best in your home. Yet you may be inclined to go with her suggestion.

Half the time you agree because you think someone else has better taste or more experience. You allow yourself to be pressured and bullied; you don't speak up and feel exasperated, later mumbling to yourself, "If only I had said no." It's time to practice saying no to those people who sway your decisions. Being impolite or terse or walking away feels much better than realizing you've been had.

Out of everyone and everything out there looking to bend you to their will, technology has made it easier for the worst offenders to take you by surprise. Electronic communication via e-mail and cell phone has opened vast, new avenues for scammers. In some cases, scammers have learned to wear "masks" so convincing that alarm bells may not even go off until it's too late. It's more common to be tricked than you may think: of fifteen thousand subjects, almost half were unable to tell whether people were lying or telling the truth. Many who pride themselves on being savvy at spotting a con when face-to-face may be tricked by a safe-looking e-mail or a curious link sent via text message. By the end of this chapter, you will be better able to navigate scammers, spot a "snow job" from a salesperson, and handle weaseling from service people.

Quiz: How Susceptible Are You to Forceful People?

We've all dealt with those who persist or invade your privacy—you know, people who, no matter what you say, don't give up, who are keen on selling, judging, or advising you. Some of us struggle to deal with forceful people more than others. When responding to the quiz, take note of what applies to you. Answering "yes," "usually," or "most of the time" may indicate that you need to adopt a firmer approach.

1. You are likely to give in if someone bothers or bugs you repeatedly.
2. If you don't fully understand something—a legal document, details of your phone contract, or what your car really needs to run properly—you're more likely to defer

to whatever is presented. You think: They're experts; they must know what they're talking about.

3. You sign up for extra services that you don't need or want because the salesperson convinced you it was a smart move.

4. After waiting weeks for the plumber to make repairs, you bend to meet his schedule even when the time is horribly inconvenient for you.

5. When shopping for new clothes, you often find yourself in a changing room full of items a salesperson assures will look good on you.

6. If you're caught off guard by an odd request, you're more likely to agree so you can move on or get it over with.

7. Fearing coming off as rude or insensitive, you find it difficult to cut off or say no to telemarketers.

8. Your gym bag is stuffed with exercise gear you probably don't need because an employee at your gym told you that you needed it to get in shape.

9. Believing the best of people, you rarely stop to consider if you're being cheated, coerced, or conned.

10. You get angry with yourself after the fact upon realizing you succumbed to someone's bullying, persistence, or assertiveness.

You have to take extra precaution to safeguard yourself at unexpected moments. The first line of defense: getting comfortable using *no*.

Selling You a Bill of Goods

Many yes-leaning people become magnets for hustlers on the prowl for a sale. Contractors tell you what to do, talking you into renovations you never considered. Telemarketers gobble your time, and salespeople are trained to sweet-talk (read:

coerce) you into owning things you don't necessarily want or need. When you get home with a purchase you were goaded into, you're disappointed with it and with yourself. Common sense tells you to refuse, to be strong, but you don't or can't. If and when you say no, the insistent don't hear you or pretend they don't.

If there weren't something in it for them, they wouldn't be asking. You have to trust yourself and your instincts to avoid being a patsy. The word *no* or simply hanging up or ignoring a sales pitch should be enough. The good thing is, while we can't always anticipate when someone will try to strong-arm us into a sale, we can have clear *no* responses ready.

··· SCENARIO ···

"If you're buying the phone to take on vacation, you really have to get this waterproof case," the salesperson says, shoving a package toward you. "Imagine you're trying to take a selfie and the phone falls into the ocean. We only have a few left. I'd grab it if I were you."

What's Going on Here: This sales rep makes all the right points and paints a realistic picture of what could happen. He's appealing to your logic, but when you see the hefty price tag, you balk. Surely you can find something that protects your purchase without breaking your wallet.

Response: "You must have other, less-expensive waterproof cases."

Alert: Not every sales or service person is out to get you, but many are.

Slick salespeople tend to show customers the most expensive merchandise first. Be skeptical of the "I only have a few left" ruse. And, always ask for alternatives before handing over your credit card.

··· SCENARIO ···

"You look smashing in that color. It complements your eyes and gives you a vibrant glow. Shall I ring you up?" the cosmetician says as you pucker your lips and move closer to the mirror.

What's Going on Here: The striking young woman behind the makeup counter slathered a new color blush on your cheeks and a provocative lipstick on your lips. In spite of what the confident beauty consultant says, you are not convinced you look all that dazzling.

Response: "No, it's really not my look."

Alert: Unlike a parent, friend, or even a coworker, you don't owe salespeople an excuse, and you certainly don't have to worry about hurting their feelings. If you are the slightest bit unsure about the makeup, the probability is high that a new blush and lipstick will be stashed unused in the back of a drawer with the heap of cosmetics you were talked into every other time you didn't say no.

··· SCENARIO ···

*You're walking your usual route to the grocery store
and see people hovering in the middle of the sidewalk.
They're wearing uniforms and holding clipboards,
obviously trying to raise money for some cause.
"Do you care about animal rights?" one asks you.*

What's Going on Here: You knew the second you saw them that
they would try to stop you. You feel bad as you see more and
more people plainly ignoring the fund-raisers, but you have
no interest in pausing your errands to listen.

Response: "No, but good luck." Or, "I care, but I can't stop
right now."

Alert: You can show you appreciate the work they do and
plainly refuse to let them hook you into their pitch. A short
response ends the conversation promptly; stopping to offer
something longer can result in your being dragged into a conversation or making a donation out of guilt. No need to add
a "Sorry."

··· SCENARIO ···

*"You'll be sorry you didn't buy this outfit. It's
so versatile. It's what everyone is wearing," the
salesperson in the sports department insists.*

What's Going on Here: Her job is to sell you—and sell you big. She's
the type who will tell you that you look great in a way-too-
skimpy bathing suit. The buyer may have bought too much
stock, and the salesperson has been instructed to push some
of the things you're trying on. She may work on commission;

the more she sells, the fatter her paycheck. She spent a long time carting different sizes and colors into a dressing room. You feel a tad obligated to buy something.

Response: "No. I'm going to think about it."

Alert: In rushing to leave an unwanted conversation or in trying to remain polite and civil, we can get pushed into conceding to another's judgment. It's okay to walk out empty-handed. Before you're on the sidewalk, she'll be with another customer. And on the remote chance that you are sorry you don't own the outfit, you can go back and buy it.

··· SCENARIO ···

"We're contractors doing work on the apartment next door, and we need to take a look at your side of the wall."

What's Going on Here: Strangers who look like workmen come to your door and appear perfectly professional—but this is the first you've heard of anyone needing to do any work on your or your neighbor's apartment.

Response: "Give me your business card. I will check with my neighbor or the super and call you tomorrow."

Alert: Even in a scenario where the workmen turn out to be legitimate, scammers rely on catching people off guard to take advantage. Be proactive by asking your neighbors to notify you in advance when they plan to have contractors working.

··· SCENARIO ···

*"Sign this retainer, and I'll get you the
money you want and then some," the
lawyer says with great confidence.*

What's Going on Here: You want to believe that he can settle your case for a lot of money and without a lengthy and stressful court trial. You suspect lawyer puffery but are intimidated by the well-appointed office and his self-assuredness. You know you should get another opinion, but how do you escape?

Response: "No, I want to think over what you're telling me." Or, "No, I'm going to see another lawyer before I decide."

Alert: Your radar should be working overtime when attorneys promise outcomes they can't predict and, for that reason, probably can't deliver.

··· SCENARIO ···

*"It's ideal, precisely what you were looking
for: enough bedrooms, good schools, large
front and back yards. You can't let this
house slip away," the Realtor urges.*

What's Going on Here: You've been house hunting for months. The agent wants to make a sale, and you want your dream house. This one isn't it, but it's close and very tempting. You start thinking about compromising (you'll live with less closet space and spend the money to renovate the kitchen), that maybe you're being too picky. Maybe what you want doesn't exist. You're relying on the Realtor's experience and knowledge of the area. You could be swayed, especially when you hear that someone else has made an offer.

Response: "You could be right, but I'll take my chances and pass on this one."

Alert: Don't worry that the real estate agent may think you are being difficult, and don't be strong-armed by the pressure of another offer. Keep looking. You'll know when you find what you want and will happily make concessions.

··· **SCENARIO** ···

"You have to drop your price if you want your house/apartment to sell."

What's Going on Here: You've studied the market and are well informed about the selling price of similar properties in the community. Given the age, condition, and location, your asking price is right, and you're willing to wait. Your Realtor isn't. The house isn't selling fast enough for him; he wants his commission now.

Response: "No, I'm holding out for my price. I'm confident I'll get it."

Alert: When you do your homework and are convinced you are on target, stick to your guns. If circumstances change and you need the money in a hurry, you can reduce your asking price when you want, not when the agent wants.

··· SCENARIO ···

"I've been watching this stock. It's as good as money in the bank. Should I buy you five hundred shares?"

What's Going on Here: You're a novice in the world of finance and inclined to trust your broker. He's done pretty well by you overall. But he also picks "dogs" and promises gains that never materialize. Until you have time to do your own investigating, put him off.

Response: "Not yet. I want to look into it first."

Alert: Beware the sure thing, because nothing is for sure in the stock market. Understand that the broker earns a commission on your buys and sells.

··· SCENARIO ···

"Trust me, everyone's ordering the sports package (video system for the kids, fancy tire rims). You can't buy a new car without it. You will be so happy you have it."

What's Going on Here: You've ordered several extras, but the salesman pushes for more. If you've done your homework before car shopping, you know your automotive must-haves.

Response: "No, thank you. What's on the list is all I'm putting in this car."

Alert: The words "trust me" or "honestly" signal the need to pay close attention. Wherever you shop, be prepared for salespeople to try to compel you to add as much as possible. If you're being pressured to buy something you didn't see as an absolute necessity before you walked in, make your *no* clear. Don't be conned by the "everyone has it" sales ploy. Everyone doesn't.

··· SCENARIO ···

"When are you going to start your package of ten training sessions?"

What's Going on Here: You finished the second of two free private classes, a sign-up bonus for joining the gym. If you don't buy the package, you worry the trainer gets nothing.

Response: "I'm going to wait to see how often I can get here and use my membership first."

Alert: The free offers are "loss leaders," also known as "come-ons"—giveaways to bring you into the gym to spend more money. Unless you want a personal trainer and have the money, don't turn a good deal—something fun and free—into a bad deal (ten sessions you don't need or can't really afford).

··· SCENARIO ···

"This is the best holiday spot in the area. It's a bargain."

What's Going on Here: The travel agent arranged a very fabulous, very glamorous vacation, but you and the agent have a very different definition of the word "bargain." The cost doesn't approximate the amount you have in your holiday budget or would ever consider spending on a trip. Much as you would like to luxuriate on a remote island and sip exotic drinks, you can't swing this extravagance.

Response: "No, it's too expensive."

Alert: Why do you care what a travel agent thinks about your discretionary spending? Remind her of the amount you allotted, get another travel person to book your holiday, or go online and book it yourself.

••• SCENARIO •••

"Yes, we had a deal, but the parts cost more.
Times are tough; I'm really hurting."

What's Going on Here: This deal maker has you marked as a softy. He'll embellish his sob story if you let him. Stories of financial woes push the guilt buttons—and pull at your heart. He may or may not be deceiving you, but that is not the issue.

Response: "No, I'm not paying additional charges. We agreed on the price."

Alert: If you bend after every sob story you hear, you'd have no money. Stop whiners with an assertive *no* before they spill their sad stories and break your resolve.

••• SCENARIO •••

An e-mail newsletter from a jewelry company
you've had your eye on for a while comes into your
inbox. The sale they're having makes you gasp:
"75 percent off. Click here for special sale link."

What's Going on Here: You've been praying for such a sale. Buyer beware. There usually is a catch—scan the fine print and you'll almost always find a gimmick of one sort or another: the deal only applies if you spend a hundred dollars or more, for instance. But still, you think that the offer may never come again.

Response: Walk away from the computer.

Alert: With so many companies announcing special sales and sending e-mail blasts, it's easy to get caught up in the need-to-have-it excitement, without thinking. In fact, marketers bank on it. The surprise promise of discounted items is purposefully designed to make buyers believe they are being responsible by not buying things at full price, to then compel you to buy more than you otherwise would.

··· SCENARIO ···

"Great news! A potential employer has selected your résumé and wants to discuss the possibility of an interview," an e-mail from a job-hunting website reads. "All we need is an exit fee and the company's full contact information will be visible."

What's Going on Here: You've been unemployed far too long and in an act of desperation, posted your résumé on more job-hunting websites than you can remember. Finally, you get a lead. But what is an "exit fee"?

Response: "Why should I have to pay a fee?" you say out loud to your computer.

Alert: There's a difference between knowing you're paying money to join more targeted, high-performance job-hunting websites and being conned into giving up some cash. This bait-and-switch tactic is a frequent one used by scammers.

Similar ones include being promised a training course for a high-paying job but first needing to pay a fee or buy into a pyramid scheme. To learn about a website company, look on consumer affairs sites or search online for postings warning of a scam—*before* getting out your credit card and making a mistake in a moment of hope.

··· SCENARIO ···

"I'm excited to inform you that you've won a free cruise!" an enthusiastic voice tells you over the phone. "To confirm our offer and grab your spot, I'll need a credit card number to hold it—you won't be charged."

What's Going on Here: The tone of the person who unexpectedly called you is friendly and warm, and her points are very convincing. It seems feasible, and a trip sounds wonderful.

Response: If it's a live person on the other end, say a curt, "No." Sometimes it's a robocall, a definite "hang up."

Alert: Don't go buying suntan lotion quite yet—if it seems too good to be true, it probably is. Best-case scenario, a legitimate explanation for the "free cruise" angel will emerge soon; worst case, you provide or punch in your credit card number and get scammed out of who knows how many dollars.

··· SCENARIO ···

*You receive an e-mail from the IRS: "We
need you to clarify information filed as part
of your most recent tax return," it reads.*

What's Going on Here: You were worried when you filed your taxes
that you didn't prepare them correctly. When you get the
e-mail, you freeze. You want to correct anything as soon as
possible. It would be a nightmare to get audited.

Response: None. The IRS advises you to not reply or click on
any links.

Alert: According to USA.gov, "The IRS does not initiate contact with a taxpayer by sending an e-mail, text, or social message requesting personal or financial information." The official
website has a place where you can report any such activity. As
with anything asking for any personal information, double-
and triple-check its legitimacy before doing anything.

··· SCENARIO ···

*"We're doing a short telephone survey. I'd
like to ask you a few questions—I'll only
take a couple minutes of your time."*

What's Going on Here: What happened to the government's no-call
list? You signed up to be sure you were through with cold calls.
Telemarketers and politicians call anyway. Some ply you with
the promise of a free trip or money if you'll listen for a minute.
Should you start to listen, the short pitch is long, the questions
too personal or too many—many more than the "short survey" the caller claimed when you answered the phone.

Response: "Take me off the list." Or simply hang up.

Alert: Intrusive telemarketers are a good place to strengthen your backbone. The chances of ever talking to the same person—or a live person—are slim. If you can't say no, hang up the phone. The caller is being rude, not you.

··· **SCENARIO** ···

You get an e-mail alert that your phone carrier needs to update your information: "Click on this link."

What's Going on Here: You immediately wonder, is this a legitimate e-mail? Why would you need to reenter all of the info when your provider already has your details? In spite of the red flags, you are tempted to respond to be done with another online request.

Response: Call the customer service line to confirm they sent the e-mail.

Alert: E-mail scams work by tricking you in a distracted moment to click on a link or download an application that could lead to malicious software taking over your phone or computer and collecting your personal information. If you fall prey, the cleanup will take up even more of your time—or worse, your money, too.

· · · · · · · · · · · ·

Getting Things Done—Your Way

Except for those jacks- and jills-of-all-trades, most of us need experts and advisors. We rely on plumbers to keep water systems in check, hairdressers and barbers to style us in ways we cannot do ourselves, and other professionals to fill in our knowledge gaps. However, the very people we need and depend on can take advantage, bully us, or give bad advice so we wind up unhappy.

When you acquiesce, you could feel angry, or possibly enraged, for shying away from a *no* and succumbing with a meek *okay*. If the babysitter runs your social calendar, the painter makes your color choices, the roofer comes only when it's convenient for him, it's time to change your ways. You are the client.

Being tough gives you some jurisdiction over the things you rely on others to do. They are trying to do their jobs, but some aren't too concerned with how the outcome or decision affects you. They proceed to the next job or customer, leaving you stewing or living with the consequences of going along with their suggestions. These questions, responses, and alerts, so typical of situations you find yourself in at one time or another, will keep you from giving in to people who can readily distress or disappoint you.

··· SCENARIO ···

"I can't start our session at 6:00 p.m.; it has to be 8:00," your child's tutor texts you the night before she was scheduled to come in. "I'm sorry to do this again! Thanks for understanding."

What's Going on Here: She's changed the schedule four times now. You said nothing because your child desperately needs her. You can't let it slide again.

Response: "This cannot keep happening. We agreed on 6:00, and the last-minute changes put my household in turmoil."

Alert: No matter how desperate you are, schedule changes are inconvenient and upsetting. Texts are useful to avoid confrontation, but a face-to-face chat when the tutor arrives will be more effective.

··· SCENARIO ···

"Something has come up. I'll have to cut our meeting short so I can get across town to another client."

What's Going on Here: You've been trying to get an appointment with this career coach for weeks. You've heard he's the best, and your friends rave about him, but you already feel completely unvalued.

Response: "I understand, but I've been waiting for weeks and do not appreciate being pushed out by another client. Let's reschedule for later this week when you won't be rushed."

Alert: Even with a big name and reputation, someone who doesn't respect clients' time can prove to be a bigger headache than a savior.

··· SCENARIO ···

"We're going to highlight your hair today," the beautician declares emphatically, as if it were a done deal. When you hesitate, she takes it a step further. "We've talked about your becoming a blonde for a long time. Let's do it," she urges.

What's Going on Here: On top of adding to your bill, maybe your stylist is having a slow day and wants to fill some time. Or maybe she really believes you will look better with highlights or hair that's two shades darker or lighter. You're not sure.

Response: "No, not today."

Alert: Even if a drastic change sounds like a good idea at the moment, wait for your next appointment so you can give the transformation some more thought to be certain it's what you want. That way, you'll avoid the shock to your system or having to avoid seeing friends until you work up the nerve to reveal what you've done.

··· SCENARIO ···

"So, I'd need to go to the store for an extra part, but I don't have time for that today. I'm going to put in this temporary patch and find a time to come back maybe next week."

What's Going on Here: Your contractor is making an inconvenience sound like it's not that big of a deal to you. You'll be the one stuck looking at the half-finished project for days while he merrily moves onto other clients. He'll come back to you when he feels like it, especially if he's been paid. You don't want to sound demanding, but you are perturbed.

Response: "No, it's important to me that this is finished today, as discussed. There has to be some way you can make that work."

Alert: Unless you say something, your contractor will assume you're okay with his pronouncement. A firm *no* will help reorder his priorities.

··· SCENARIO ···

*"The color warms up the room.
It's perfect. I went ahead and finished."*

What's Going on Here: Your instructions to the painter had been explicit: put a sample on the wall near the kitchen. He forged ahead and will try to convince you that you love it—even though instantly you hate it. He'll insist he can't change it— it's too late, the room is done, that'll cost extra—and will assure you that you'll get used to it.

Response: "No, it's not what I want. I can't live with it."

Alert: He's wrong; you are right. Don't back down. If you do, you will be reminded every time you enter the room of how you allowed him to browbeat you.

··· SCENARIO ···

*"I can't break up the set. We never do that,"
the antique dealer tells you when you
spot a platter and pitcher, part of a
grouping that includes dinner plates.*

What's Going on Here: In large stores and chain stores there may be little room for bartering. Small shops or flea markets are another story. In life, there are exceptions. Walk away or be firm.

Response: "No. I don't want the set. I want those two pieces."

Alert: The dealer wants you to believe that there's no room for negotiation. "Always" and "never" are fictional situations that don't exist; that may explain why we have the expression "never say never." When you no longer seem interested, you stand a better chance of leaving with what you want.

··· SCENARIO ···

"We need to operate immediately—within the next two weeks." The doctor frowns to underscore the urgency he feels. "I know what I'm talking about," he adds to remind you that he's the authority.

What's Going on Here: You're terrified by the illness and cowed by the doctor's experience and reputation. Friends whose medical opinion you trust said he's the best in his specialty. The symptoms are complicated and could mean a different diagnosis, one with cure options other than surgery. The doctor says he's positive his diagnosis is correct and tells you he has an opening in his surgery schedule for next Wednesday. You are meant to feel lucky that he can squeeze you in.

Response: "No, I want to get a second opinion; it will probably agree with yours."

Alert: You've massaged his ego, so he'll welcome you back to schedule the surgery if that is your decision, but it will be an informed one. Competent doctors don't object to patients consulting with other doctors.

··· SCENARIO ···

"Please add your social security number under your signature," the mover asks as the last of your furniture is loaded on the truck.

249

What's Going on Here: The moving company representative insists the company cannot hold your items in storage without your social security number. With identity theft rampant, you don't want your social security number on papers the movers will plop on the seat of their truck for anyone to see. You can't fathom why they need it.

Response: "Absolutely not. Get a supervisor on the phone."

Alert: Going over someone's head, known as "escalating the call or contact," tends to get the result or answer you want.

··· SCENARIO ···

*"If you open a store credit card account,
I can give you an additional 10 percent off,"
the sales person at the register informs you.*

What's Going on Here: You are buying a coat, the one you've been searching for and wanted and it's on sale. The salesperson is sweetening an already good deal and it's hard to resist an additional discount. But, you have a hard and fast rule to limit your number of credit cards.

Response: "I don't use store credit cards. Never will."

Alert: Credit cards often carry high interest rates and hidden penalties that may not be obvious. Sometimes it's a hassle to close an account. The monthly bill, whether or not you buy anything, is another thing you would need to keep on your radar.

··· SCENARIO ···

"This is one of the best mother-daughter photo shoots I've ever done," the photographer e-mails, to your delight. "Can I include some of the shots on my website?"

What's Going on Here: Browsing this photographer's past work online convinced you to hire her to photograph you and your young daughter in the first place. You paid a hefty amount but don't feel the need to help market her business. You are a very private person.

Response: "I love the work you did but don't feel comfortable having our pictures go public. Perhaps next time."

Alert: You can be a good client without feeling you owe the photographer a favor. You're likely not the first client to say no.

. . . .

Out-of-the-Blue Challenges

We all know what it's like to be hit with impolite comments out of left field. Strangers who butt into your personal business over the Internet or in public present sometimes hidden yet very real ways to unnerve you. Unexpected impositions can feel like attacks from people you don't know. Those who attempt to influence you can be the most jarring. Reproach hurts, especially when you are not sure if what you are doing is right.

Keep your responses sparse and don't apologize for being uncooperative. Don't think it's polite to be cooperative and listen to what the person says. Say no to suggestions that make you uncomfortable, angry, or suspicious. The more personal the "judgment," the more acceptable it is to be abrupt.

••• SCENARIO •••

"Your baby is adorable," a woman at the mall coos as she observes you bottle-feeding your infant. Then, she hands you a pamphlet and adds, "Breast is best. You're actually doing damage right now."

What's Going on Here: You already know exactly what the pamphlet says and will throw it out. You went through painful, disappointing conversations with your doctor before deciding that bottle-feeding was the best option. The stranger doesn't know you or your story.

Response: "No, I don't need that. Please leave us alone."

Alert: Uncalled-for meddling doesn't deserve a friendly response.

••• SCENARIO •••

"It's a simple do-it-yourself project. The baby will spend hours playing with the mobile you made. You can do it," one mother assures you in an encouraging tone.

What's Going on Here: You joined a new mom's group to get some social time for the baby and adult interaction for yourself. What you got instead was more guilt about your mothering. After two meetings you feel shamed and inadequate. The mothers exude Pinterest perfection, challenge you with advice, and prod you to venture into areas that are not your long suit.

Response: "I don't think so. I'm not artistic or crafty in any way."

Alert: Motherhood unpacks a tremendous amount of guilt without any outside input. Stay away from people who make your feel insecure about your skills or ability to be a good parent.

··· SCENARIO ···

"Your dress looks stunning on you. I know I shouldn't ask, but what did it cost? (What diet are you on? Is that the real thing or a knockoff?)"

What's Going on Here: A complete stranger randomly asks a personal question. Does she want your genetic history and your social security number, too? You don't want to answer, but you also don't want to look like a jerk by cutting the interaction short.

Response: "Thanks, but I don't remember." Or, "I'm in a hurry." Or, "I'd rather not say."

Alert: A stranger may mean well, but if you're not comfortable speaking about your body or your shopping habits, that's okay.

··· SCENARIO ···

Another parent in the pediatrician's office starts chatting with you: "Is yours an only child?" You nod. "You need to give her a sibling soon if you want them to be close growing up."

What's Going on Here: You're used to family members and friends questioning your choice to raise a singleton, but a perfect stranger is a new experience.

Response: "We're a perfectly happy family with one. If you'll excuse me, but we're going to go back to our book (game, puzzle)."

Alert: A blunt reply should feel about right for those nervy enough to interfere, even if the question raises or reawakens doubts you may have. Only you and your partner should weigh in on family size decisions, not random people in doctors' waiting rooms, the grocery store, or playground. Cut them off.

··· SCENARIO ···

"Would you switch seats so I can be with my friend?" the airline passenger next to you asks from her middle seat. She's pointing to her friend a row back who is also in a dreaded middle seat, waving and smiling at you.

What's Going on Here: You booked an aisle seat for a fairly lengthy trip, maybe even paid extra for it. If it were a parent wanting to sit next to his toddler or young child or an older person who you felt needed her companion, you probably would seriously consider moving. These women look to be perfectly healthy millennials.

Response: "Why don't you ask a flight attendant if she can help you?" Or, "I don't change seats. I think it's bad luck."

Alert: Couples will also often ask for your seat so they can sit together. Couple status doesn't rank over a single person's status. And, some people will try almost anything to get your seat—from feigning illness to offering to buy you drinks. You don't have to be miserable for the duration of a flight or feel guilty about remaining in the seat you selected.

··· SCENARIO ···

"How come you decided to adopt?"

What's Going on Here: Your family and closest friends don't ask. Here, someone you met recently or possibly a few hours ago wants the intimate details of your reproductive history. Far too personal and rude!

Response: "Way too complicated to get into."

Alert: When questions are this intrusive, feel free to give a snarky answer. If you want to be polite, a simple "I don't care to talk about it" will get the person to stop because he or she is expecting the full story.

··· SCENARIO ···

"Wow! What a rock. How much did that thing cost?"

What's Going on Here: Waiting your turn at the cleaners, the person behind you gets nosy. Sure, you enjoy wearing your engagement ring, but it's not an open invitation for a chat. Plus, you don't want to draw attention to your pricey piece of jewelry.

Response: "I'm not sure." Or, "I'd rather not say."

Alert: A curt yet civil response could help the asker realize the audacity of her question.

··· SCENARIO ···

Strangers appear at your doorstep. "We were driving by and noticed you were adding on another story. We're thinking of doing the same thing. Can we see your plans?"

What's Going on Here: They ask before introducing themselves or asking your name.

Response: "Let me get you our architect's e-mail and phone number. I'm sure he will be happy to help you."

Alert: You paid for your architectural plans. They may be blinded by their eagerness or just shameless freeloaders.

··· SCENARIO ···

"I have to ask. What race are you? Your look is so unusual—stunning really."

What's Going on Here: People have been asking you this question your entire life. The prying about your ethnicity makes you feel more like an object than a human.

Response: "It's a very long story that I'm not going into."

Alert: It's okay to brush off very personal questions that make you uncomfortable, even if the asker flatters you or seems genuinely interested.

··· SCENARIO ···

"Excuse me, but is that your child? He looks much too young to be climbing all over the jungle gym like that. He's going to hurt my children. Can he get off by himself?"

What's Going on Here: You and your son are at his favorite playground spot. He knows it well. He may look smaller than the other kids, but you are perfectly confident in his abilities.

Response: "He's capable. I'm keeping an eye on him."

Alert: Only you know what's safe for your child.

··· SCENARIO ···

"How can you leave your child with that dog?" a passerby says. "Don't you know anything about pit bulls?"

What's Going on Here: You're on a daily walk around the park with your toddler and trusty pit bull, Roxy, and ran to the other end of the path to throw something in the trash. You raised your dog from a pup and know she stands guard by the stroller when you step away. Roxy is an ideal nanny dog, but you endure censure from those who take frightening news reports about pit bulls as gospel.

Response: You want to say, "Mind your own business," but contain your outrage and say, "It's okay; I know my dog."

Alert: When someone protests your behavior, maintain a calm demeanor, but be clear.

Your New Mind-Set

You've seen them do it—triumphant athletes pumping their arms in elation at their successes. When you say no, you'll feel like raising your arms like a champion and shouting, "Yesss!" Saying no often enough secures your boundaries, preserves your time, and maintains focus on your goals.

Think of each "Should I?" or "Shouldn't I?" as a practice session. Like any other skill, the first few times are hard, but at least you are trying, and that's progress from your usual impulsive, agreeable self. In short order, turning people down will become noticeably less difficult. You will find that making *no* more of a habit is freeing, joyful.

Finding the Courage

Keep your antenna up and running, on the alert for people who attempt to cross the boundaries you put in place. If *no* runs through your mind upon hearing a request, if instinctively that's how you want to respond, find the moxie to go with the feeling. Not everyone asking something from you expects you to say yes—certainly not all the time. When you are assertive and stand up for yourself, people are reluctant to ask. Because most people don't like to be refused, they will avoid asking. It's human nature.

Consider the people you don't ask favors from and ask yourself why that is. It's probably because they have said no to you in the past. When you need strength or the incentive to say no, remember the friends, relatives, and coworkers who have little trouble saying no to you. Make them your benchmark, your source of courage. In spite of the times they failed to do a favor or turned down what you thought was a reasonable request, they remain in your inner circle. Most likely you still like, respect, or admire them.

At this point have the courage to retire your guilt and feel good about every *no* you utter. Guilt is a wasted emotion; it eats up time and is almost never worth the drain on the psyche. Without guilt, you'll be able to focus on critical and important responsibilities and ignore the unimportant. Your parent isn't coming home to punish you because you didn't do what you were told—at least not anymore!

Saying Yes to the *No* Word

Sometimes it takes being trapped to mark your territory, but start practicing until you can call up a *no* when you want it. You may falter at times, but don't be too hard on yourself. The person you said yes to will be back at some point, and you'll be ready to say no.

Refusing is not easy, and sometimes it's downright uncomfortable, but saying yes habitually creates a combination of anxiety, anger, stress, regret, and feelings of powerlessness. That's why it's important to keep your priorities straight. Know what you want so you don't forgo your needs.

When your resistance fails or you feel burdened, these thoughts and mantras will shore you up and have you reaching for that *no* with less effort. They are crucial reinforcement to keep you focused on your goals and priorities so you can accomplish more of what you want and less of what others want from you.

Read and reread as needed:

- The first *no* to a person makes subsequent refusals easier.

- The word *no* or its equivalent is enough. Lengthy explanations leave room for debate, misinterpretation, or permission to ask again.
- Less is more. The less said in the way of excuses, the stronger the message.
- Don't apologize for being unavailable.
- Be leery of people who assume you consent.
- Be sure the person asking is in your friend, family, or elite work circle before weighing how or if you want to comply.
- Having a reputation for being the person everyone leans on is not flattering and makes you a prime target for being railroaded into more yeses.
- If you're known for being able to juggle many tasks at once or for doing everything well, play down that reputation. Being a star performer simply begets more requests.
- When possible, anticipate what will be asked. Thinking ahead of time about possible situations that may arise enables you to decide what you are willing to do.
- Agreeing to do what others ask doesn't make you a nicer person.
- Being buttoned up, enthusiastic, or willing is great within limits, but don't overdo the image.
- You can't do enough for some people, so don't try.
- You are not responsible for the problems others create for themselves, and you can't singlehandedly make them happy.
- Dissect each request carefully to make sure you are not being bribed, cajoled, bullied, or threatened.
- Before agreeing to anything, ask yourself if you have the time.

- Be aware of your limits; reconsider and redefine your boundaries to ease an escape.
- Believe that you can say no and remain an involved, caring, and committed person.
- Say no with conviction. Look the person in the eye to let him or her know you mean it, that appeals and pressure are useless.
- Don't fret over the consequences of refusing. The fallout is never as severe or damaging as you think; more likely it's absent or insignificant.
- Most people understand and forgive. You don't want unforgiving people in your life anyway.
- Prompt yourself daily: saying no is liberating and it's your right.

If you expend too much energy looking for approval, worrying about how others perceive you, being a do-gooder, or overly compensating as payback to those who helped you, you leave little time to take care of yourself—to rest, work out, read, see movies, be with your children, spend time with your partner, or maybe fall in love. Use available time to connect with those who make you laugh, who make you happy—time you won't have if you are at the beck and call of those who continually seek you out, especially those who think the world revolves around them.

When you understand that most people aren't thinking about you, aren't worrying about what you think, and many times aren't concerned with how you will feel, you'll be less hesitant to say no. Store this thought toward the back of your mind: he or she is not thinking about me. With that thought tucked away, you become more discriminating about doling out assistance.

When a close family member is distraught or ill and needs support, you will want to extend yourself. When a friend is going through a rough time or a colleague must tend to a personal crisis, a natural drive takes over and propels you to do what you can do. You'll be there to help in any way you can. Special and extenuating circumstances should be exceptions, not part of haphazard commitments and responsibilities you used to assume far too frequently.

The *No* Credo

The *No* Credo provides the ammunition to short-circuit those who believe they can impose on you. If you slip into old yes-patterns, don't agonize. Refer to this credo—your Bill of Rights—as a reminder of the freedom and life you deserve.

You have the right to:

- Keep your plans and needs in the forefront so that saying no is possible.
- Establish and guard your personal boundaries.
- Make your feelings and desires known.
- Use *no* to get your life in order and to be in control of it.
- Exercise your power and choice to say no. You almost always have a choice.
- Think "No" before you think, "No problem, I'll do that for you."
- Say no initially and change your mind later if you wish.
- Request the details before committing.
- Alter a request to make it—or part of it—manageable.
- Avoid tasks beyond your ability or expertise.
- Turn down those who flatter or attempt to pressure you into a *yes*.
- Postpone an answer; stalling for time is your prerogative.
- Refuse anyone who insists on an immediate answer.

- Withhold explanations in an attempt to soften your *no*.
- Suggest someone else or offer an alternative solution.
- Save "I'm sorry" for when you have actually done something wrong.

Bowing Out: Your New Mind-Set

A *no* education inoculates you against the people-pleasing "disease." You've learned how, when, and why to reclaim *no* and put it back in your vocabulary, to make it the preferred response. That single word relieves a tremendous amount of life's tension, stress, and aggravation. You'll like yourself better when the days of being other people's scaffolding—their perpetual support system—are long gone.

The reality is, whatever you say yes to will eventually force you to say no to something you really want to do or someone you really want to help. When giving out time and services, be selective so you can say yes to the people you truly want to assist.

You now have a reservoir of different ways to say no and a better grasp of what and whom to say no to. You'll be able to stop the persuasive people who ask too much, too often. You'll stop volunteering indiscriminately and start to think about askers' motives before you commit. Processing requests—that is, analyzing them before you jump to a *yes* response—eliminates the inner conflict and disappointment you feel after you agree.

Saying no means making a conscious effort—choosing—to be in charge of your life. Begin today, if you haven't already. Doing so moves *you* to the front of the line of people you want to please, and that's exactly where you belong.

About the Authors

Susan Newman, PhD is a social psychologist and author. Her research and writing focus on parenting and family relationship issues. She is the author of more than a dozen books and a regular contributor to *Psychology Today* and *US News & World Report*. Her work has been featured in *The New York Times*, *USA Today*, *The Washington Post* as well as in numerous other newspapers and national magazines. She appears on major news outlets, among them, CNN, NPR, *Good Morning America*, *The Today Show*, and *CBS Sunday Morning* to discuss breaking news, social trends, and parenting concerns.

Dr. Newman is a member of the American Psychological Association, the Authors Guild, and the American Society of Journalists and Authors. She is a Court-Appointed Special Advocate (CASA) for abused and neglected children.

She lives in the New York Metro area and is the mother of one son and four stepchildren. Visit her website at www.susannewmanphd.com.

Cristina Schreil is an award-winning journalist and photojournalist and ghostwriter of two parenting books. She covers many cultural topics and contributes to several magazines both online and in print. Visit her website at www. cristinaschreil.com.

Thank you for reading *The Book of No*. Please share your thoughts in a review at http://amzn.to/2qAz1B0.